DEAD HE LAY THERE IN THE SUNSET.

# THE

# SONG OF HIAWATHA

BY

HENRY WADSWORTH LONGFELLOW

WITH INTRODUCTION

BY

NATHAN HASKELL DOLE

———

NEW YORK: 46 EAST 14TH STREET

## THOMAS Y. CROWELL & COMPANY

BOSTON: 100 PURCHASE STREET

TYPOGRAPHY BY C. J. PETERS & SON, BOSTON.

PRESSWORK BY BERWICK & SMITH.

# INTRODUCTION.

(TO HIAWATHA.)

---

The Finns, or Suomi, who were perhaps the earliest immigrants into Europe from their aboriginal home in Asia, possess an epic, the *Kalevala*, consisting, in the edition published by Dr. Lönnrot in 1842, of about twenty-three thousand lines. Dr. Max Müller declares that it "will claim its place as the fifth national epic of the world, side by side with the *Ionian Songs*, with the *Mahābhārata*, the *Shah' nāmeh* and the *Nibelungen.*" Grimm places Dr. Lönnrot, as its collector, with Homer, Vergil, the singer of the *Nibelungenlied*, and Camões. It is comparable with the national verse of Spain, and it is interesting to remember that the Basques, the earliest inhabitants of Spain, are kin to the Finns.

The *Kalevala*, so called from the national name of Finland, meaning "Land of Heroes," is composed throughout in eight-syllable trochaic [1] verses, varied by repetitions, by musical alliterations, and often by a succession of rimes.

---

[1] Trochaic dimeter catalectic.

Longfellow knew the German translation, and had laughed with Ferdinand Freiligrath "over the pages of the *Finnische Runen*" a dozen years before he noted in his diary, under date of June 5, 1854, that he was reading with great delight the Finnish epic *Kalevala*, and added: "It is charming." It evidently suggested not only the measure, but also the plan, of a poem that should weave together into a whole the beautiful legends and traditions of the American Indians. At first he proposed to call it *Manabozho;* but before the month was fairly over he had decided to call it *Hiawatha*, which, he says, was another name for the same personage.[1] Though he obtained many suggestions as to personages and incidents from the three "ill-digested" quartos of Schoolcraft, and also read Tanner, Heckewelder, and other authorities, he confided to his diary that it was "purely in the realm of fancy." The hero he called "a kind of American Prometheus."

The last canto was finished on March 21, 1855, at noon; and the first edition of five thousand copies, of which four thousand were sold in advance, was issued on Nov. 10. By the first of January it was selling at the rate of three hundred copies a day, and in a year and a quarter upwards of fifty thousand copies had been distributed. Its success in England was not less remarkable. Longfellow's friends were enthusiastic in its praise. Emerson

[1] See Appendix.

found it "very wholesome, sweet and wholesome as maize, very proper and pertinent for us to read, and showing a kind of manly sense of duty in the poet to write." Bayard Taylor wrote: "The imagery is wonderfully apt and descriptive, and the whole poem floats in an atmosphere of the American Indian summer." But he thought the measure too sportive — "possibly tender and pathetic, but not passionate;" he ended with the prediction that it would live after the Indian race had vanished from our continent.

Its reception by the press was generally flattering; though some critics followed in the footsteps of Poe, and charged him with plagiarism. There can be no doubt that he was strongly influenced by the Finnish epic. Read these introductory lines, translated by John Martin Crawford, and the resemblance cannot fail to strike: —

> Golden friend, and dearest brother,
> Brother dear of mine in childhood,
> Come and sing with me the stories,
> Come and chant with me the legends,
> Legends of the times forgotten,
> Since we now are here together,
> Come together from our roamings.
> Seldom do we come for singing,
> Seldom to the one the other,
> O'er this cold and cruel country,
> O'er the poor soil of the Northland.
> Let us clasp our hands together

That we thus may best remember.
Join we now in merry singing,
Chant we now the oldest folk-lore,
That the dear ones all may hear them,
That the well-inclined may hear them,
Of this rising generation.
These are words in childhood taught me,
Songs preserved from distant ages;
Legends they that once were taken
From the belt of Wainamoinen,
From the forge of Ilmarinen,
From the sword of Kaukomieli,
From the bow of Youkahainen,
From the pastures of the Northland,
From the meads of Kalevala.
These my dear old father sang me
When at work with knife and hatchet:
These my tender mother taught me
When she twirled the flying spindle,
When a child upon the matting
By her feet I rolled and tumbled.
Incantations were not wanting
Over Sampo and o'er Louhi,
Sampo growing old in singing,
Louhi ceasing her enchantment.
In the songs died wise Wipunen,
At the games died Lemmikainen.
There are many other legends,
Incantations that were taught me,
That I found along the wayside,
Gathered in the fragrant copses,
Blown me from the forest branches,
Culled among the plumes of pine-trees,
Scented from the vines and flowers,
Whispered to me as I followed
Flocks in land of honeyed meadows,

Over hillocks green and golden,
After sable-haired Murikki,
And the many-colored Kimmo.
Many runes the cold has told me,
Many lays the rain has brought me,
Other songs the winds have sung me:
Many birds from many forests
Oft have sung me lays in concord;
Waves of sea and ocean billows,
Music from the many waters,
Music from the whole creation,
Oft have been my guide and master.
Sentences the trees created,
Rolled together into bundles,
Moved them to my ancient dwelling,
On the sledges to my cottage,
Tied them to my garret rafters,
Hung them on my dwelling-portals,
Laid them in a chest of boxes,
Boxes lined with shining copper.
Long they lay within my dwelling,
Through the chilling winds of winter,
In my dwelling-place for ages.
Shall I bring these songs together?

.   .   .   .   .   .   .

It will add to our enchantment,
To the pleasure of the evening,
Northland's long and dreary evening,
For the beauty of the day-dawn,
For the pleasure of the morning,
The beginning of the new day.

Here are the last fourteen lines in the original
Suomi: —

Lauloaksemme hywiä,
Parahia paunaksemme,
Kuulla noien kultaisien,
Tietä mieletehtoisien,
Nuorisossa nousewassa,
Kansassa kasuawassa,
Noita saamia sanoja,
Wirsiä wirittämiä.
Wyöltäwanhan Wäinämöisen,
Alta ahjon Ilmarisen,
Päästä kaluan Kaukomielen
Joukahaisen, jousen tiestä
Pohjan peltojen periltä
Kalewalan kankahilta.

The literal translation runs : —

Let us sing delightfully — let us give of our best — that our
friends may listen — let eager minds hear us — let the growing
youths — let the old — hear these borrowed words — these songs
gathered from — the old Wäinämöinen's girdle — from under
the forge of Ilmarinen [1] — from Kaukomieli's sword-point —
from Jukahainen, bow — from the Northland country — from
the sand-hills of Kaleva's home.[2]

---

[1] Ilmarinen, God of the Wind, like Mudjekeewis, father of Hiawatha.

[2] M. A. Castrén's Swedish version of the last lines goes : —

Sångens vänner dem förnimma
Bland den ungdom, nu här uppgår,
Bland den skara, som här växer —
Dessa ord som gåfva fångna,
Dessa ljufva sånger, tagna
Från den gamle Wäinös bälte,
Under Ilmarinen's ässja,
Ned från Kaukomieles svärdsudd,
Joukahainens båges bane

When Hiawatha, who is the son of Mudjekeewis,
goes to see how fares it with his father, —

> "At the door-ways of the West-Wind,
> At the portals of the Sunset,

old Nokomis warns him, saying, —

> "Go not forth, O Hiawatha!
> To the Kingdom of the West-Wind,
> To the realms of Mudjekeewis,
> Lest he harm you with his magic,
> Lest he kill you with his cunning."

So in the third rune of the *Kalevala*, when the

> Från det innersta af Pohja
> Och från Kalevalas moar.

The lines, —

> Niinlaulan hywänkiwirren
> Kaunihinki kalkuttelen,
> Rusalta rukihiselta,
> Uluelta ohraiselta,

are translated by Anton Scheifner: —

> Werd' ein hübsches Lied so singen,
> Dass es wunderschön ertöne
> Von dem Bier das ich genossen,
> Von dem schönen Gerstentranke—

The same in the wonderfully skilful Hungarian version of Barna
Ferdinand read: —

> Szép dalt fogom én zengeni,
> Szép verseket énikelni.
> A jeles rosz eledeltöl,
> A jó izü árpa sörtöl.

And in the later Swedish version of Collan: —

> Så en vacker sång jag sjunger
> Låter goda runor ljuda,
> Sen med rågbröd mig jag mättot
> Och förplägat mig med korn-öl.

young and reckless minstrel of Lapland, Youkahainen —

> " Vows that he will Northward hasten,
>    Hie him Northward and betake him
>    To the dwellings of Wainola,
>    To the cabins of the Northland,
>    There as bard to vie in battle
>    With the famous Wainamoinen," —

Wainamoinen being the son of the Storm-Wind and
Ilmatar, the Beauteous Daughter of the Air, the Lapland mother cries, —

> " Go not hence to Wainamoinen,
>    There with him to offer battle ;
>    He will charm thee with his singing,
>    Will bewitch thee in his anger,
>    He will drive thee back dishonored,
>    Sink thee in the fatal snow-drift,
>    Turn to ice thy pliant fingers,
>    Turn to ice thy feet and ankles."

   Then one may compare the passing of Hiawatha
at the very end of the last canto with the departure
of Wainomoinen in the rune of Mariatta : —

> " As the years passed, Wainamoinen
>    Recognized his waning powers :
>    Empty-handed, heavy-hearted,
>    Sang his farewell song to Northland,
>    To the people of Wainola ;
>    Sang himself a boat of copper.
>    Beautiful his bark of magic ;
>    At the helm sat the magician,
>    Sat the ancient wisdom-singer.
>    Westward, westward sailed the hero.

O'er the blue-black of the waters,
Singing as he left Wainola.
This his plaintive song and echo:—
'Songs may rise and set in Suomi,
Rise and set for generations,
When the North will learn my teachings,
Will recall my wisdom sayings,
Hungry for the true religion.
Then will Suomi need my coming,
Watch for me at dawn of morning,
That I may bring back the Sampo,
Bring anew the harp of joyance,
Bring again the golden moonlight,
Bring again the silver sunshine,
Peace and plenty to the Northland.'
　　Thus the ancient Wainamoinen,
In his copper-banded vessel,
Left his tribe in Kalevala,
Sailing o'er the rolling billows,
Sailing through the azure vapors,
Sailing through the dusk of evening,
Sailing to the fiery sunset,
To the higher-landed regions,
To the lower verge of heaven;
Quickly gained the far horizon,
Gained the purple-colored harbor.
There his bark he firmly anchored,
Rested in his boat of copper.
But he left his harp of magic,
Left his songs and wisdom-sayings,
To the lasting joy of Suomi."

Any one not familiar with the Kalevala, and re-
membering Hiawatha as a song long sung, would
infallibly, on hearing those lines read, attribute them

to Longfellow. The experiment has been tried. We must also in all fairness recognize that the translator of the *Kalevala* would perhaps be to a certain extent influenced in his phraseology by the language of *Hiawatha*. But it is not extravagant to claim that, just as Vergil imitated Homer, so Longfellow, more or less consciously, imitated the Suomi epic; nor does it detract from the value or interest of the American poem. The metre is particularly well adapted to the presentation of the Indian legends; the names glide easily into the lilting, monotonous measure, and it would be difficult, even if it were desirable, to avoid the quaint repetitions so characteristic of these two poems.

It must be remembered that the genius of the English language looks somewhat askance upon the trochaic measure, and is far more at home with the statelier iambics. And it was a bold venture to compose so long a poem in this alien form. It is not strange that some of the lines limp as if they were tired of going so fast. Longfellow himself felt that it was a risky experiment, and his diary records some of his friends' comments on it as he read it to them in the course of its creation. Thus, about six months after he had fairly begun it, he records the expression of a friend's fears that it will lack human interest, and adds that he must put a live, beating human heart into it.

A little before he chronicles his misgivings, and

at the same time his absorption in the theme. That he managed to put the live human heart into it is evidenced by its perennial popularity and by the fact that it has outlived all the innumerable travesties that grew up about it and threatened to choke out its life. It has been translated into various languages, and has served at least two generations of schoolboys for declamations on the platform. It may be justly regarded as the national epic of the Indian race — the one tribute that the Muses have rendered to offset all the abuses which the white race have imposed on their predecessors.

In order that the reader may see what basis Longfellow had for his Indian subject, and may appreciate what a service the poet renders in lifting legends into the realm of fancy, a few selections from Schoolcraft's *Algic Researches*, and from his great work on the Indians, have been added in an appendix. It will be seen how the magic touch transmutes the crude material of the Indian folk tale into the finished, graceful poem that appeals to the heart of the most cultivated, and yet has the fragrance of the primitive woods. Such was Longfellow's triumph, and the passage of long years has only intensified the admiration of the world for his masterpiece.

NATHAN HASKELL DOLE.

BOSTON, *Feb.* 18, 1898.

# CONTENTS.

# THE SONG OF HIAWATHA.

## INTRODUCTION.

SHOULD you ask me, whence these stories?
Whence these legends and traditions,
With the odors of the forest,
With the dew and damp of meadows,
With the curling smoke of wigwams,
With the rushing of great rivers,
With their frequent repetitions,
And their wild reverberations,
As of thunder in the mountains?

I should answer, I should tell you:—
"From the forests and the prairies,
From the great lakes of the Northland,
From the land of the Ojibways,
From the land of the Dacotahs,
From the mountains, moors, and fen-lands,

1

Where the heron, the Shuh-shuh-gah,
Feeds among the reeds and rushes.
I repeat them as I heard them
From the lips of Nawadaha,
The musician, the sweet singer."

Should you ask where Nawadaha
Found these songs, so wild and wayward,
Found these legends and traditions,
I should answer, I should tell you: —
"In the bird's-nests of the forest,
In the lodges of the beaver,
In the hoof-prints of the bison,
In the eyry of the eagle!

"All the wild-fowl sang them to him,
In the moorlands and the fen-lands,
In the melancholy marshes;
Chetowaik, the plover, sang them,
Mahng, the loon, the wild goose, Wawa,
The blue heron, the Shuh-shuh-gah,
And the grouse, the Mushkodasa!"

If still further you should ask me,
Saying, "Who was Nawadaha?
Tell us of this Nawadaha,"
I should answer your inquiries

Straightway in such words as follow.

"In the Vale of Tawasentha,
In the green and silent valley,
By the pleasant water-courses,
Dwelt the singer Nawadaha.
Round about the Indian village
Spread the meadows and the corn-fields,
And beyond them stood the forest,
Stood the groves of singing pine-trees,
Green in Summer, white in Winter,
Ever sighing, ever singing.

"And the pleasant water-courses,
You could trace them through the valley,
By the rushing in the Spring-time,
By the alders in the Summer,
By the white fog in the Autumn,
By the black line in the Winter;
And beside them dwelt the singer,
In the Vale of Tawasentha,
In the green and silent valley.

"There he sang of Hiawatha,
Sang the Song of Hiawatha,
Sang his wondrous birth and being,
How he prayed and how he fasted,

How he lived, and toiled, and suffered,
That the tribes of men might prosper,
That he might advance his people!"

    Ye who love the haunts of Nature,
Love the sunshine of the meadow,
Love the shadow of the forest,
Love the wind among the branches,
And the rain-shower and the snow-storm,
And the rushing of great rivers
Through their palisades of pine-trees,
And the thunder in the mountains,
Whose innumerable echoes
Flap like eagles in their eyries; —
Listen to these wild traditions,
To this Song of Hiawatha!

    Ye who love a nation's legends,
Love the ballads of a people,
That like voices from afar off
Call to us to pause and listen,
Speak in tones so plain and childlike,
Scarcely can the ear distinguish
Whether they are sung or spoken; —
Listen to this Indian Legend,
To this Song of Hiawatha!

Ye whose hearts are fresh and simple,
Who have faith in God and Nature,
Who believe, that in all ages
Every human heart is human,
That in even savage bosoms
There are longings, yearnings, strivings
For the good they comprehend not,
That the feeble hands and helpless,
Groping blindly in the darkness,
Touch God's right hand in that darkness
And are lifted up and strengthened;—
Listen to this simple story,
To this Song of Hiawatha!

Ye, who sometimes, in your rambles
Through the green lanes of the country,
Where the tangled barberry-bushes
Hang their tufts of crimson berries
Over stone walls gray with mosses,
Pause by some neglected graveyard,
For a while to muse, and ponder
On a half-effaced inscription,
Written with little skill of song-craft,
Homely phrases, but each letter
Full of hope and yet of heart-break,

Full of all the tender pathos
Of the Here and the Hereafter; —
Stay and read this rude inscription,
Read this Song of Hiawatha!

# I.

## THE PEACE-PIPE.

On the Mountains of the Prairie,
On the great Red Pipe-stone Quarry,
Gitche Manito, the mighty,
He the Master of Life, descending,
On the red crags of the quarry
Stood erect, and called the nations,
Called the tribes of men together.

From his footprints flowed a river,
Leaped into the light of morning,
O'er the precipice plunging downward
Gleamed like Ishkoodah, the comet.
And the Spirit, stooping earthward,
With his finger on the meadow
Traced a winding pathway for it,
Saying to it: — "Run in this way!"
From the red stone of the quarry

With his hand he broke a fragment,
Moulded it into a pipe-head,
Shaped and fashioned it with figures;
From the margin of the river
Took a long reed for a pipe-stem,
With its dark green leaves upon it;
Filled the pipe with bark of willow,
With the bark of the red willow;
Breathed upon the neighboring forest,
Made its great boughs chafe together,
Till in flame they burst and kindled;
And erect upon the mountains,
Gitche Manito, the mighty,
Smoked the calumet, the Peace-Pipe,
As a signal to the nations.

And the smoke rose slowly, slowly,
Through the tranquil air of morning,
First a single line of darkness,
Then a denser, bluer vapor,
Then a snow-white cloud unfolding,
Like the tree-tops of the forest,
Ever rising, rising, rising,
Till it touched the top of heaven,
Till it broke against the heaven,

And rolled outward all around it.
  From the Vale of Tawasentha,
From the Valley of Wyoming,
From the groves of Tuscaloosa,
From the far-off Rocky Mountains,
From the Northern lakes and rivers,
All the tribes beheld the signal,
Saw the distant smoke ascending,
The Pukwana of the Peace-Pipe.

  And the Prophets of the nations
Said: — "Behold it, the Pukwana!
By this signal from afar off,
Bending like a wand of willow,
Waving like a hand that beckons,
Gitche Manito, the mighty,
Calls the tribes of men together,
Calls the warriors to his council!"

  Down the rivers, o'er the prairies,
Came the warriors of the nations,
Came the Delawares and Mohawks,
Came the Choctaws and Camanches,
Came the Shoshonies and Blackfeet,
Came the Pawnees and Omawhaws,
Came the Mandans and Dacotahs,

Came the Hurons and Ojibways,
All the warriors drawn together
By the signal of the Peace-Pipe,
To the Mountains of the Prairie,
To the great Red Pipe-stone Quarry.

    And they stood there on the meadow,
With their weapons and their war-gear,
Painted like the leaves of Autumn,
Painted like the sky of morning,
Wildly glaring at each other;
In their faces stern defiance,
In their hearts the feuds of ages,
The hereditary hatred,
The ancestral thirst of vengeance.

    Gitche Manito, the mighty,
The creator of the nations,
Looked upon them with compassion,
With paternal love and pity;
Looked upon their wrath and wrangling
But as quarrels among children,
But as feuds and fights of children!

    Over them he stretched his right hand,
To subdue their stubborn natures,
To allay their thirst and fever,

By the shadow of his right hand;
Spake to them with voice majestic
As the sound of far-off waters,
Falling into deep abysses,
Warning, chiding, spake in this wise:—

"O my children! my poor children!
Listen to the words of wisdom,
Listen to the words of warning,
From the lips of the Great Spirit,
From the Master of Life, who made you!

"I have given you lands to hunt in,
I have given you streams to fish in,
I have given you bear and bison,
I have given you roe and reindeer,
I have given you brant and beaver,
Filled the marshes full of wild-fowl,
Filled the rivers full of fishes;
Why then are you not contented?
Why then will you hunt each other?

"I am weary of your quarrels,
Weary of your wars and bloodshed,
Weary of your prayers for vengeance,
Of your wranglings and dissensions;
All your strength is in your union,

All your danger is in discord;
Therefore be at peace henceforward,
And as brothers live together.

"I will send a Prophet to you,
A Deliverer of the nations,
Who shall guide you and shall teach you,
Who shall toil and suffer with you.
If you listen to his counsels,
You will multiply and prosper;
If his warnings pass unheeded,
You will fade away and perish!

"Bathe now in the stream before you,
Wash the war-paint from your faces,
Wash the blood-stains from your fingers,
Bury your war-clubs and your weapons,
Break the red stone from this quarry,
Mould and make it into Peace-Pipes,
Take the reeds that grow beside you,
Deck them with your brightest feathers,
Smoke the calumet together,
And as brothers live henceforward!"

Then upon the ground the warriors
Threw their cloaks and shirts of deer-skin,
Threw their weapons and their war-gear,

Leaped into the rushing river,
Washed the war-paint from their faces.
Clear above them flowed the water,
Clear and limpid from the footprints
Of the Master of Life descending;
Dark below them flowed the water,
Soiled and stained with streaks of crimson,
As if blood were mingled with it!

From the river came the warriors,
Clean and washed from all their war-paint;
On the banks their clubs they buried,
Buried all their warlike weapons.
Gitche Manito, the mighty,
The Great Spirit, the creator,
Smiled upon his helpless children!

And in silence all the warriors
Broke the red stone of the quarry,
Smoothed and formed it into Peace-Pipes,
Broke the long reeds by the river,
Decked them with their brightest feathers,
And departed each one homeward,
While the Master of Life, ascending,
Through the opening of cloud-curtains,
Through the doorways of the heaven,

Vanished from before their faces,
In the smoke that rolled around him,
The Pukwana of the Peace-Pipe!

## II.

### THE FOUR WINDS.

"Honor be to Mudjekeewis!"
Cried the warriors, cried the old men,
When he came in triumph homeward
With the sacred Belt of Wampum,
From the regions of the North-Wind,
From the kingdom of Wabasso,
From the land of the White Rabbit.

He had stolen the Belt of Wampum
From the neck of Mishe-Mokwa,
From the Great Bear of the mountains,
From the terror of the nations,
As he lay asleep and cumbrous
On the summit of the mountains,
Like a rock with mosses on it,
Spotted brown and gray with mosses.

Silently he stole upon him,

Till the red nails of the monster
Almost touched him, almost scared him,
Till the hot breath of his nostrils
Warmed the hands of Mudjekeewis,
As he drew the Belt of Wampum
Over the round ears, that heard not,
Over the small eyes, that saw not,
Over the long nose and nostrils,
The black muffle of the nostrils,
Out of which the heavy breathing
Warmed the hands of Mudjekeewis.

Then he swung aloft his war-club,
Shouted loud and long his war-cry,
Smote the mighty Mishe-Mokwa
In the middle of the forehead,
Right between the eyes he smote him.

With the heavy blow bewildered,
Rose the Great Bear of the mountains;
But his knees beneath him trembled,
And he whimpered like a woman,
As he reeled and staggered forward,
As he sat upon his haunches;
And the mighty Mudjekeewis,
Standing fearlessly before him,

Taunted him in loud derision,
Spake disdainfully in this wise: —
"Hark you, Bear! you are a coward,
And no Brave, as you pretended;
Else you would not cry and whimper
Like a miserable woman!
Bear! you know our tribes are hostile,
Long have been at war together;
Now you find that we are strongest,
You go sneaking in the forest,
You go hiding in the mountains!
Had you conquered me in battle
Not a groan would I have uttered;
But you, Bear! sit here and whimper,
And disgrace your tribe by crying,
Like a wretched Shaugodaya,
Like a cowardly old woman!"

Then again he raised his war-club,
Smote again the Mishe-Mokwa
In the middle of his forehead,
Broke his skull, as ice is broken
When one goes to fish in Winter.
Thus was slain the Mishe-Mokwa,
He the Great Bear of the mountains,

He the terror of the nations.
  "Honor be to Mudjekeewis!"
With a shout exclaimed the people,
"Honor be to Mudjekeewis!
Henceforth he shall be the West-Wind,
And hereafter and for ever
Shall he hold supreme dominion
Over all the winds of heaven.
Call him no more Mudjekeewis,
Call him Kabeyun, the West-Wind!"

  Thus was Mudjekeewis chosen
Father of the Winds of Heaven.
For himself he kept the West-Wind,
Gave the others to his children;
Unto Wabun gave the East-Wind,
Gave the South to Shawondasee,
And the North-Wind, wild and cruel,
To the fierce Kabibonokka.

  Young and beautiful was Wabun;
He it was who brought the morning,
He it was whose silver arrows
Chased the dark o'er hill and valley;
He it was whose cheeks were painted
With the brightest streaks of crimson,

And whose voice awoke the village,
Called the deer, and called the hunter.

Lonely in the sky was Wabun;
Though the birds sang gayly to him,
Though the wild-flowers of the meadow
Filled the air with odors for him,
Though the forests and the rivers
Sang and shouted at his coming,
Still his heart was sad within him,
For he was alone in heaven.

But one morning, gazing earthward,
While the village still was sleeping,
And the fog lay on the river,
Like a ghost, that goes at sunrise,
He beheld a maiden walking
All alone upon a meadow,
Gathering water-flags and rushes
By a river in the meadow.

Every morning, gazing earthward,
Still the first thing he beheld there
Was her blue eyes looking at him,
Two blue lakes among the rushes.
And he loved the lonely maiden,
Who thus waited for his coming;

For they both were solitary,
She on earth and he in heaven.

And he wooed her with caresses,
Wooed her with his smile of sunshine,
With his flattering words he wooed her,
With his sighing and his singing,
Gentlest whispers in the branches,
Softest music, sweetest odors,
Till he drew her to his bosom,
Folded in his robes of crimson,
Till into a star he changed her,
Trembling still upon his bosom ;
And for ever in the heavens
They are seen together walking,
Wabun and the Wabun-Annung,
Wabun and the Star of Morning.

But the fierce Kabibonokka
Had his dwelling among icebergs.
In the everlasting snow-drifts,
In the kingdom of Wabasso,
In the land of the White Rabbit.
He it was whose hand in Autumn
Painted all the trees with scarlet,
Stained the leaves with red and yellow;

He it was who sent the snow-flakes,
Sifting, hissing through the forest,
Froze the ponds, the lakes, the rivers,
Drove the loon and sea-gull southward,
Drove the cormorant and heron
To their nests of sedge and sea-tang
In the realms of Shawondasee.

Once the fierce Kabibonokka
Issued from his lodge of snow-drifts,
From his home among the icebergs,
And his hair, with snow besprinkled,
Streamed behind him like a river,
Like a black and wintry river,
As he howled and hurried southward,
Over frozen lakes and moorlands.

There among the reeds and rushes
Found he Shingebis, the diver,
Trailing strings of fish behind him,
O'er the frozen fens and moorlands,
Lingering still among the moorlands,
Though his tribe had long departed
To the land of Shawondasee.

Cried the fierce Kabibonokka,
"Who is this that dares to brave me?

Dares to stay in my dominions,
When the Wawa has departed,
When the wild-goose has gone southward,
And the heron, the Shuh-shuh-gah,
Long ago departed southward?
I will go into his wigwam,
I will put his smouldering fire out!"

    And at night Kabibonokka
To the lodge came wild and wailing,
Heaped the snow in drifts about it,
Shouted down into the smoke-flue,
Shook the lodge-poles in his fury,
Flapped the curtain of the door-way.
Shingebis, the diver, feared not,
Shingebis, the diver, cared not;
Four great logs had he for fire-wood,
One for each moon of the winter,
And for food the fishes served him.
By his blazing fire he sat there,
Warm and merry, eating, laughing,
Singing, "O Kabibonokka,
You are but my fellow-mortal!"

    Then Kabibonokka entered,
And though Shingebis, the diver,

Felt his presence by the coldness,
Felt his icy breath upon him,
Still he did not cease his singing,
Still he did not leave his laughing,
Only turned the log a little,
Only made the fire burn brighter,
Made the sparks fly up the smoke-flue.

  From Kabibonokka's forehead,
From his snow-besprinkled tresses,
Drops of sweat fell fast and heavy,
Making dints upon the ashes,
As along the eaves of lodges,
As from drooping boughs of hemlock,
Drips the melting snow in spring-time,
Making hollows in the snow-drifts.

  Till at last he rose defeated,
Could not bear the heat and laughter,
Could not bear the merry singing,
But rushed headlong through the door-way,
Stamped upon the crusted snow-drifts,
Stamped upon the lakes and rivers,
Made the snow upon them harder,
Made the ice upon them thicker,
Challenged Shingebis, the diver,

To come forth and wrestle with him,
To come forth and wrestle naked
On the frozen fens and moorlands.

 Forth went Shingebis, the diver,
Wrestled all night with the North-Wind,
Wrestled naked on the moorlands
With the fierce Kabibonokka,
Till his panting breath grew fainter,
Till his frozen grasp grew feebler,
Till he reeled and staggered backward,
And retreated, baffled, beaten,
To the kingdom of Wabasso,
To the land of the White Rabbit,
Hearing still the gusty laughter,
Hearing Shingebis, the diver,
Singing, "O Kabibonokka,
You are but my fellow-mortal!"

 Shawondasee, fat and lazy,
Had his dwelling far to southward,
In the drowsy, dreamy sunshine,
In the never-ending Summer.
He it was who sent the wood-birds,
Sent the Opechee, the robin,
Sent the blue-bird, the Owaissa,

Sent the Shawshaw, sent the swallow,
Sent the wild-goose, Wawa, northward,
Sent the melons and tobacco,
And the grapes in purple clusters.

From his pipe the smoke ascending
Filled the sky with haze and vapor,
Filled the air with dreamy softness,
Gave a twinkle to the water,
Touched the rugged hills with smoothness,
Brought the tender Indian Summer,
In the Moon when nights are brightest,
In the dreary moon of Snow-shoes.

Listless, careless Shawondasee!
In his life he had one shadow,
In his heart one sorrow had he.
Once, as he was gazing northward,
Far away upon a prairie
He beheld a maiden standing,
Saw a tall and slender maiden
All alone upon a prairie;
Brightest green were all her garments,
And her hair was like the sunshine.

Day by day he gazed upon her,
Day by day he sighed with passion,

Day by day his heart within him
Grew more hot with love and longing
For the maid with yellow tresses.
But he was too fat and lazy
To bestir himself and woo her;
Yes, too indolent and easy
To pursue her and persuade her.
So he only gazed upon her,
Only sat and sighed with passion
For the maiden of the prairie.

Till one morning, looking northward,
He beheld her yellow tresses
Changed and covered o'er with whiteness,
Covered as with whitest snow-flakes.
"Ah! my brother from the North-land,
From the kingdom of Wabasso,
From the land of the White Rabbit!
You have stolen the maiden from me,
You have laid your hand upon her,
You have wooed and won my maiden,
With your stories of the North-land!"

Thus the wretched Shawondasee
Breathed into the air his sorrow;
And the South-Wind o'er the prairie

Wandered warm with sighs of passion,
With the sighs of Shawondasee,
Till the air seemed full of snow-flakes,
Full of thistle-down the prairie,
And the maid with hair like sunshine
Vanished from his sight for ever;
Never more did Shawondasee
See the maid with yellow tresses!

Poor, deluded Shawondasee!
'T was no woman that you gazed at,
'T was no maiden that you sighed for,
'T was the prairie dandelion
That through all the dreamy Summer
You had gazed at with such longing,
You had sighed for with such passion,
And had puffed away for ever,
Blown into the air with sighing.
Ah! deluded Shawondasee!

Thus the Four Winds were divided;
Thus the sons of Mudjekeewis
Had their stations in the heavens,
At the corners of the heavens;
For himself the West-Wind only
Kept the mighty Mudjekeewis.

## III.

### HIAWATHA'S CHILDHOOD.

DOWNWARD through the evening twilight,
In the days that are forgotten,
In the unremembered ages,
From the full moon fell Nokomis,
Fell the beautiful Nokomis,
She a wife, but not a mother.

She was sporting with her women,
Swinging in a swing of grape-vines,
When her rival, the rejected,
Full of jealousy and hatred,
Cut the leafy swing asunder,
Cut in twain the twisted grape-vines,
And Nokomis fell affrighted
Downward through the evening twilight,
On the Muskoday, the meadow,
On the prairie full of blossoms.

" See! a star falls!" said the people ;
" From the sky a star is falling!"
    There among the ferns and mosses,
There among the prairie lilies,
On the Muskoday, the meadow,
In the moonlight and the starlight,
Fair Nokomis bore a daughter.
And she called her name Wenonah,
As the first-born of her daughters.
And the daughter of Nokomis
Grew up like the prairie lilies,
Grew a tall and slender maiden,
With the beauty of the moonlight,
With the beauty of the starlight.
    And Nokomis warned her often,
Saying oft, and oft repeating,
" O, beware of Mudjekeewis,
Of the West-Wind, Mudjekeewis ;
Listen not to what he tells you ;
Lie not down upon the meadow,
Stoop not down among the lilies,
Lest the West-Wind come and harm you!"
    But she heeded not the warning,
Heeded not those words of wisdom,

And the West-Wind came at evening,
Walking lightly o'er the prairie,
Whispering to the leaves and blossoms,
Bending low the flowers and grasses,
Found the beautiful Wenonah,
Lying there among the lilies,
Wooed her with his words of sweetness,
Wooed her with his soft caresses,
Till she bore a son in sorrow,
Bore a son of love and sorrow.

Thus was born my Hiawatha,
Thus was born the child of wonder;
But the daughter of Nokomis,
Hiawatha's gentle mother,
In her anguish died deserted
By the West-Wind, false and faithless,
By the heartless Mudjekeewis.

For her daughter, long and loudly
Wailed and wept the sad Nokomis;
"O that I were dead!" she murmured,
"O that I were dead, as thou art!
No more work, and no more weeping,
Wahonomin! Wahonomin!"

By the shores of Gitche Gumee,

By the shining Big-Sea-Water,
Stood the wigwam of Nokomis,
Daughter of the Moon, Nokomis.
Dark behind it rose the forest,
Rose the black and gloomy pine-trees,
Rose the firs with cones upon them;
Bright before it beat the water,
Beat the clear and sunny water,
Beat the shining Big-Sea-Water.

   There the wrinkled, old Nokomis
Nursed the little Hiawatha,
Rocked him in his linden cradle,
Bedded soft in moss and rushes,
Safely bound with reindeer sinews;
Stilled his fretful wail by saying,
"Hush! the Naked Bear will get thee!"
Lulled him into slumber, singing,
"Ewa-yea! my little owlet!
Who is this, that lights the wigwam?
With his great eyes lights the wigwam?
Ewa-yea! my little owlet!"

   Many things Nokomis taught him
Of the stars that shine in heaven;
Showed him Ishkoodah, the comet,

Ishkoodah, with fiery tresses;
Showed the Death-Dance of the spirits,
Warriors with their plumes and war-clubs,
Flaring far away to northward
In the frosty nights of Winter;
Showed the broad, white road in heaven,
Pathway of the ghosts, the shadows,
Running straight across the heavens,
Crowded with the ghosts, the shadows.

At the door on summer evenings
Sat the little Hiawatha;
Heard the whispering of the pine-trees,
Heard the lapping of the water,
Sounds of music, words of wonder;
"Minne-wawa!" said the pine-trees,
"Mudway-aushka!" said the water.

Saw the fire-fly, Wah-wah-taysee,
Flitting through the dusk of evening,
With the twinkle of its candle
Lighting up the brakes and bushes,
And he sang the song of children,
Sang the song Nokomis taught him:
"Wah-wah-taysee, little fire-fly,
Little, flitting, white-fire insect,

Little, dancing, white-fire creatures
Light me with your little candle,
Ere upon my bed I lay me,
Ere in sleep I close my eyelids!"

Saw the moon rise from the water
Rippling, rounding from the water,
Saw the flecks and shadows on it,
Whispered, "What is that, Nokomis?"
And the good Nokomis answered:
"Once a warrior, very angry,
Seized his grandmother, and threw her
Up into the sky at midnight;
Right against the moon he threw her;
'T is her body that you see there."

Saw the rainbow in the heaven,
In the eastern sky, the rainbow,
Whispered, "What is that, Nokomis?"
And the good Nokomis answered:
"'T is the heaven of flowers you see there;
All the wild-flowers of the forest,
All the lilies of the prairie,
When on earth they fade and perish,
Blossom in that heaven above us."

When he heard the owls at midnight,

Hooting, laughing in the forest,
"What is that?" he cried in terror;
"What is that?" he said, "Nokomis?"
And the good Nokomis answered:
"That is but the owl and owlet,
Talking in their native language,
Talking, scolding at each other."
   Then the little Hiawatha
Learned of every bird its language,
Learned their names and all their secrets,
How they built their nests in Summer,
Where they hid themselves in Winter,
Talked with them whene'er he met them,
Called them "Hiawatha's Chickens."

   Of all beasts he learned the language,
Learned their names and all their secrets,
How the beavers built their lodges,
Where the squirrels hid their acorns,
How the reindeer ran so swiftly,
Why the rabbit was so timid,
Talked with them whene'er he met them,
Called them "Hiawatha's Brothers."

   Then Iagoo, the great boaster,
He the marvellous story-teller,

He the traveller and the talker,
He the friend of old Nokomis,
Made a bow for Hiawatha;
From a branch of ash he made it,
From an oak-bough made the arrows,
Tipped with flint, and winged with feathers,
And the cord he made of deer-skin.

Then he said to Hiawatha:
"Go, my son, into the forest,
Where the red deer herd together,
Kill for us a famous roebuck,
Kill for us a deer with antlers!"

Forth into the forest straightway
All alone walked Hiawatha
Proudly, with his bow and arrows;
And the birds sang round him, o'er him,
"Do not shoot us, Hiawatha!"
Sang the Opechee, the robin,
Sang the blue-bird, the Owaissa,
"Do not shoot us, Hiawatha!"

Up the oak-tree, close beside him,
Sprang the squirrel, Adjidaumo,
In and out among the branches,
Coughed and chattered from the oak-tree,

Laughed, and said between his laughing,
"Do not shoot me, Hiawatha!"

And the rabbit from his pathway
Leaped aside, and at a distance
Sat erect upon his haunches,
Half in fear and half in frolic,
Saying to the little hunter,
"Do not shoot me, Hiawatha!"

But he heeded not, nor heard them,
For his thoughts were with the red deer;
On their tracks his eyes were fastened,
Leading downward to the river,
To the ford across the river,
And as one in slumber walked he.

Hidden in the alder-bushes,
There he waited till the deer came,
Till he saw two antlers lifted,
Saw two eyes look from the thicket,
Saw two nostrils point to windward,
And a deer came down the pathway,
Flecked with leafy light and shadow
And his heart within him fluttered,
Trembled like the leaves above him,
Like the birch-leaf palpitated,

As the deer came down the pathway.
 Then, upon one knee uprising,
Hiawatha aimed an arrow;
Scarce a twig moved with his motion,
Scarce a leaf was stirred or rustled,
But the wary roebuck started,
Stamped with all his hoofs together,
Listened with one foot uplifted,
Leaped as if to meet the arrow;
Ah! the singing, fatal arrow,
Like a wasp it buzzed and stung him!

 Dead he lay there in the forest,
By the ford across the river;
Beat his timid heart no longer,
But the heart of Hiawatha
Throbbed and shouted and exulted,
As he bore the red deer homeward,
And Iagoo and Nokomis
Hailed his coming with applauses.

 From the red deer's hide Nokomis
Made a cloak for Hiawatha,
From the red deer's flesh Nokomis
Made a banquet in his honor.
All the village came and feasted,

All the guests praised Hiawatha,
Called him Strong-Heart, Soan-ge-taha!
Called him Loon-Heart, Mahn-go-taysee!

## IV.

#### HIAWATHA AND MUDJEKEEWIS.

Out of childhood into manhood
Now had grown my Hiawatha,
Skilled in all the craft of hunters,
Learned in all the lore of old men,
In all youthful sports and pastimes,
In all manly arts and labors.

Swift of foot was Hiawatha;
He could shoot an arrow from him,
And run forward with such fleetness,
That the arrow fell behind him!
Strong of arm was Hiawatha;
He could shoot ten arrows upward,
Shoot them with such strength and swiftness,
That the tenth had left the bow-string
Ere the first to earth had fallen!

He had mittens, Minjekahwun,

Magic mittens made of deer-skin;
When upon his hands he wore them,
He could smite the rocks asunder,
He could grind them into powder.
He had moccasins enchanted,
Magic moccasins of deer-skin;
When he bound them round his ankles,
When upon his feet he tied them,
At each stride a mile he measured!

Much he questioned old Nokomis
Of his father Mudjekeewis;
Learned from her the fatal secret
Of the beauty of his mother,
Of the falsehood of his father;
And his heart was hot within him,
Like a living coal his heart was.

Then he said to old Nokomis,
"I will go to Mudjekeewis,
See how fares it with my father,
At the doorways of the West-Wind,
At the portals of the Sunset!"

From his lodge went Hiawatha,
Dressed for travel, armed for hunting;
Dressed in deer-skin shirt and leggings,

Richly wrought with quills and wampum;
On his head his eagle-feathers,
Round his waist his belt of wampum,
In his hand his bow of ash-wood,
Strung with sinews of the reindeer;
In his quiver oaken arrows,
Tipped with jasper, winged with feathers;
With his mittens, Minjekahwun,
With his moccasons enchanted.

Warning said the old Nokomis,
"Go not forth, O Hiawatha!
To the kingdom of the West-Wind,
To the realms of Mudjekeewis,
Lest he harm you with his magic,
Lest he kill you with his cunning!"

But the fearless Hiawatha
Heeded not her woman's warning;
Forth he strode into the forest,
At each stride a mile he measured;
Lurid seemed the sky above him,
Lurid seemed the earth beneath him,
Hot and close the air around him,
Filled with smoke and fiery vapors,
As of burning woods and prairies,

For his heart was hot within him,
Like a living coal his heart was.

  So he journeyed westward, westward,
Left the fleetest deer behind him,
Left the antelope and bison;
Crossed the rushing Esconawbaw,
Crossed the mighty Mississippi,
Passed the Mountains of the Prairie,
Passed the land of Crows and Foxes,
Passed the dwellings of the Blackfeet,
Came unto the Rocky Mountains,
To the kingdom of the West-Wind,
Where upon the gusty summits
Sat the ancient Mudjekeewis,
Ruler of the winds of heaven.

  Filled with awe was Hiawatha
At the aspect of his father.
On the air about him wildly
Tossed and streamed his cloudy tresses,
Gleamed like drifting snow his tresses,
Glared like Ishkoodah, the comet,
Like the star with fiery tresses.

  Filled with joy was Mudjekeewis
When he looked on Hiawatha,

Saw his youth rise up before him
In the face of Hiawatha,
Saw the beauty of Wenonah
From the grave rise up before him.

"Welcome!" said he, "Hiawatha,
To the kingdom of the West-Wind!
Long have I been waiting for you!
Youth is lovely, age is lonely,
Youth is fiery, age is frosty;
You bring back the days departed,
You bring back my youth of passion,
And the beautiful Wenonah!"

Many days they talked together,
Questioned, listened, waited, answered;
Much the mighty Mudjekeewis
Boasted of his ancient prowess,
Of his perilous adventures,
His indomitable courage,
His invulnerable body.

Patiently sat Hiawatha,
Listening to his father's boasting;
With a smile he sat and listened,
Uttered neither threat nor menace,
Neither word nor look betrayed him,

But his heart was hot within him,
Like a living coal his heart was.

Then he said, "O Mudjekeewis,
Is there nothing that can harm you?
Nothing that you are afraid of?"
And the mighty Mudjekeewis,
Grand and gracious in his boasting,
Answered, saying, "There is nothing,
Nothing but the black rock yonder,
Nothing but the fatal Wawbeek!"

And he looked at Hiawatha
With a wise look and benignant,
With a countenance paternal,
Looked with pride upon the beauty
Of his tall and graceful figure,
Saying, "O my Hiawatha!
Is there anything can harm you?
Anything you are afraid of?"

But the wary Hiawatha
Paused awhile, as if uncertain,
Held his peace, as if resolving,
And then answered, "There is nothing,
Nothing but the bulrush yonder,
Nothing but the great Apukwa!"

And as Mudjekeewis, rising,
Stretched his hand to pluck the bulrush,
Hiawatha cried in terror,
Cried in well-dissembled terror,
"Kago! kago! do not touch it!"
"Ah, kaween!" said Mudjekeewis,
"No indeed, I will not touch it!"
  Then they talked of other matters;
First of Hiawatha's brothers,
First of Wabun, of the East-Wind,
Of the South-Wind, Shawondasee,
Of the North, Kabibonokka;
Then of Hiawatha's mother,
Of the beautiful Wenonah,
Of her birth upon the meadow,
Of her death, as old Nokomis
Had remembered and related.
  And he cried, "O Mudjekeewis,
It was you who killed Wenonah,
Took her young life and her beauty,
Broke the Lily of the Prairie,
Trampled it beneath your footsteps;
You confess it! you confess it!"
And the mighty Mudjekeewis

Tossed his gray hairs to the West-Wind,
Bowed his hoary head in anguish,
With a silent nod assented.

　Then up started Hiawatha,
And with threatening look and gesture
Laid his hand upon the black rock,
On the fatal Wawbeek laid it,
With his mittens, Minjekahwun,
Rent the jutting crag asunder,
Smote and crushed it into fragments,
Hurled them madly at his father,
The remorseful Mudjekeewis,
For his heart was hot within him,
Like a living coal his heart was.

　But the ruler of the West-Wind
Blew the fragments backward from him,
With the breathing of his nostrils,
With the tempest of his anger,
Blew them back at his assailant;
Seized the bulrush, the Apukwa,
Dragged it with its roots and fibres
From the margin of the meadow,
From its ooze, the giant bulrush;
Long and loud laughed Hiawatha!

Then began the deadly conflict,
Hand to hand among the mountains;
From his eyrie screamed the eagle,
The Keneu, the great War-Eagle;
Sat upon the crags around them,
Wheeling flapped his wings above them.

Like a tall tree in the tempest
Bent and lashed the giant bulrush;
And in masses huge and heavy
Crashing fell the fatal Wawbeek;
Till the earth shook with the tumult
And confusion of the battle,
And the air was full of shoutings,
And the thunder of the mountains,
Starting, answered, "Baim-wawa!"

Back retreated Mudjekeewis,
Rushing westward o'er the mountains,
Stumbling westward down the mountains,
Three whole days retreated fighting,
Still pursued by Hiawatha
To the doorways of the West-Wind,
To the portals of the Sunset,
To the earth's remotest border,
Where into the empty spaces

Sinks the sun, as a flamingo
Drops into her nest at nightfall,
In the melancholy marshes.

"Hold!" at length cried Mudjekeewis,
"Hold, my son, my Hiawatha!
'T is impossible to kill me,
For you cannot kill the immortal.
I have put you to this trial,
But to know and prove your courage;
Now receive the prize of valor!

"Go back to your home and people,
Live among them, toil among them,
Cleanse the earth from all that harms it,
Clear the fishing-grounds and rivers,
Slay all monsters and magicians,
All the giants, the Wendigoes,
All the serpents, the Kenabeeks,
As I slew the Mishe-Mokwa,
Slew the Great Bear of the mountains.

"And at last when Death draws near you,
When the awful eyes of Pauguk
Glare upon you in the darkness,
I will share my kingdom with you,
**Ruler** shall you be thenceforward

Of the Northwest-Wind, Keewaydin,
Of the home-wind, the Keewaydin."

Thus was fought that famous battle
In the dreadful days of Shah-shah,
In the days long since departed,
In the kingdom of the West-Wind.
Still the hunter sees its traces
Scattered far o'er hill and valley;
Sees the giant bulrush growing
By the ponds and water-courses,
Sees the masses of the Wawbeek
Lying still in every valley.

Homeward now went Hiawatha;
Pleasant was the landscape round him,
Pleasant was the air above him,
For the bitterness of anger
Had departed wholly from him,
From his brain the thought of vengeance,
From his heart the burning fever.

Only once his pace he slackened,
Only once he paused or halted,
Paused to purchase heads of arrows
Of the ancient Arrow-maker,
In the land of the Dacotahs,

Where the Falls of Minnehaha
Flash and gleam among the oak-trees,
Laugh and leap into the valley.

There the ancient Arrow-maker
Made his arrow-heads of sandstone,
Arrow-heads of chalcedony,
Arrow-heads of flint and jasper,
Smoothed and sharpened at the edges,
Hard and polished, keen and costly.

With him dwelt his dark-eyed daughter,
Wayward as the Minnehaha,
With her moods of shade and sunshine,
Eyes that smiled and frowned alternate,
Feet as rapid as the river,
Tresses flowing like the water,
And as musical a laughter;
And he named her from the river,
From the water-fall he named her,
Minnehaha, Laughing Water.

Was it then for heads of arrows,
Arrow-heads of chalcedony,
Arrow-heads of flint and jasper,
That my Hiawatha halted
In the land of the Dacotahs?

Was it not to see the maiden,
See the face of Laughing Water
Peeping from behind the curtain,
Hear the rustling of her garments
From behind the waving curtain,
As one sees the Minnehaha
Gleaming, glancing through the branches,
As one hears the Laughing Water
From behind its screen of branches?

Who shall say what thoughts and visions
Fill the fiery brains of young men?
Who shall say what dreams of beauty
Filled the heart of Hiawatha?
All he told to old Nokomis,
When he reached the lodge at sunset,
Was the meeting with his father,
Was his fight with Mudjekeewis;
Not a word he said of arrows,
Not a word of Laughing Water!

## V.

### HIAWATHA'S FASTING.

You shall hear how Hiawatha
Prayed and fasted in the forest,
Not for greater skill in hunting,
Not for greater craft in fishing,
Not for triumphs in the battle,
And renown among the warriors,
But for profit of the people,
For advantage of the nations.

First he built a lodge for fasting,
Built a wigwam in the forest,
By the shining Big-Sea-Water,
In the blithe and pleasant Spring-time,
In the Moon of Leaves he built it,
And, with dreams and visions many,
Seven whole days and nights he fasted.

On the first day of his fasting

Through the leafy woods he wandered;
Saw the deer start from the thicket,
Saw the rabbit in his burrow,
Heard the pheasant, Bena, drumming,
Heard the squirrel, Adjidaumo,
Rattling in his hoard of acorns,
Saw the pigeon, the Omeme,
Building nests among the pine-trees,
And in flocks the wild goose, Wawa,
Flying to the fen-lands northward,
Whirring, wailing far above him.
"Master of Life!" he cried, desponding,
"Must our lives depend on these things?"
On the next day of his fasting
By the river's brink he wandered,
Through the Muskoday, the meadow,
Saw the wild rice, Mahnomonee,
Saw the blueberry, Meenahga,
And the strawberry, Odahmin,
And the gooseberry, Shahbomin,
And the grape-vine, the Bemahgut,
Trailing o'er the alder-branches,
Filling all the air with fragrance!
"Master of Life!" he cried, desponding,

"Must our lives depend on these things?"
    On the third day of his fasting
By the lake he sat and pondered,
By the still, transparent water;
Saw the sturgeon, Nahma, leaping,
Scattering drops like beads of wampum,
Saw the yellow perch, the Sahwa,
Like a sunbeam in the water,
Saw the pike, the Maskenozha,
And the herring, Okahahwis,
And the Shawgashee, the craw-fish!
"Master of Life!" he cried, desponding,
"Must our lives depend on these things?"
    On the fourth day of his fasting
In his lodge he lay exhausted;
From his couch of leaves and branches
Gazing with half-open eyelids,
Full of shadowy dreams and visions,
On the dizzy, swimming landscape,
On the gleaming of the water,
On the splendor of the sunset.
    And he saw a youth approaching,
Dressed in garments green and yellow,
Coming through the purple twilight,

Through the splendor of the sunset;
Plumes of green bent o'er his forehead,
And his hair was soft and golden.

Standing at the open doorway,
Long he looked at Hiawatha,
Looked with pity and compassion
On his wasted form and features,
And, in accents like the sighing
Of the South-Wind in the tree-tops,
Said he: — O my Hiawatha!
All your prayers are heard in heaven,
For you pray not like the others,
Not for greater skill in hunting,
Not for greater craft in fishing,
Not for triumph in the battle,
Nor renown among the warriors,
But for profit of the people,
For advantage of the nations.

"From the Master of Life descending,
I, the friend of man, Mondamin,
Come to warn you and instruct you,
How by struggle and by labor
You shall gain what you have prayed for.
Rise up from your bed of branches,

Rise, O youth, and wrestle with me!"
  Faint with famine, Hiawatha
Started from his bed of branches,
From the twilight of his wigwam
Forth into the flush of sunset
Came, and wrestled with Mondamin;
At his touch he felt new courage
Throbbing in his brain and bosom,
Felt new life and hope and vigor
Run through every nerve and fibre.

  So they wrestled there together
In the glory of the sunset,
And the more they strove and struggled,
Stronger still grew Hiawatha;
Till the darkness fell around them,
And the heron, the Shuh-shuh-gah,
From her haunts among the fen-lands,
Gave a cry of lamentation,
Gave a scream of pain and famine.
"'T is enough!" then said Mondamin,
Smiling upon Hiawatha,
"But to-morrow when the sun sets,
I will come again to try you."
And he vanished, and was seen not;

Whether sinking as the rain sinks,
Whether rising as the mists rise,
Hiawatha saw not, knew not,
Only saw that he had vanished,
Leaving him alone and fainting,
With the misty lake below him,
And the reeling stars above him.

On the morrow and the next day,
When the sun through heaven descending,
Like a red and burning cinder
From the hearth of the Great Spirit,
Fell into the western waters,
Came Mondamin for the trial,
For the strife with Hiawatha;
Came as silent as the dew comes,
From the empty air appearing,
Into empty air returning,
Taking shape when earth it touches,
But invisible to all men
In its coming and its going.

Thrice they wrestled there together
In the glory of the sunset,
Till the darkness fell around them,
Till the heron, the Shuh-shuh-gah,

From her haunts among the fen-lands,
Uttered her loud cry of famine,
And Mondamin paused to listen.

Tall and beautiful he stood there,
In his garments green and yellow;
To and fro his plumes above him
Waved and nodded with his breathing,
And the sweat of the encounter
Stood like drops of dew upon him.

And he cried: — "O Hiawatha!
Bravely have you wrestled with me,
Thrice have wrestled stoutly with me,
And the Master of Life, who sees us,
He will give to you the triumph!"

Then he smiled, and said: — "To-morrow
Is the last day of your conflict,
Is the last day of your fasting,
You will conquer and o'ercome me;
Make a bed for me to lie in,
Where the rain may fall upon me,
Where the sun may come and warm me;
Strip these garments, green and yellow,
Strip this nodding plumage from me,
Lay me in the earth, and make it

Soft and loose and light above me.

"Let no hand disturb my slumber,
Let no weed nor worm molest me,
Let not Kahgahgee, the raven,
Come to haunt me and molest me,
Only come yourself to watch me,
Till I wake, and start, and quicken,
Till I leap into the sunshine."

And thus saying, he departed;
Peacefully slept Hiawatha,
But he heard the Wawonaissa,
Heard the whippoorwill complaining,
Perched upon his lonely wigwam;
Heard the rushing Sebowisha,
Heard the rivulet rippling near him,
Talking to the darksome forest;
Heard the sighing of the branches,
As they lifted and subsided
At the passing of the night-wind,
Heard them, as one hears in slumber
Far-off murmurs, dreamy whispers:
Peacefully slept Hiawatha.

On the morrow came Nokomis,
On the seventh day of his fasting,

Came with food for Hiawatha,
Came imploring and bewailing,
Lest his hunger should o'ercome him,
Lest his fasting should be fatal.

But he tasted not, and touched not,
Only said to her: — " Nokomis,
Wait until the sun is setting,
Till the darkness falls around us,
Till the heron, the Shuh-shuh-gah,
Crying from the desolate marshes,
Tells us that the day is ended."

Homeward weeping went Nokomis,
Sorrowing for her Hiawatha,
Fearing lest his strength should fail him,
Lest his fasting should be fatal.
He meanwhile sat weary waiting
For the coming of Mondamin,
Till the shadows, pointing eastward,
Lengthened over field and forest,
Till the sun dropped from the heaven,
Floating on the waters westward,
As a red leaf in the Autumn
Falls and floats upon the water,
Falls and sinks into its bosom.

And behold! the young Mondamin,
With his soft and shining tresses,
With his garments green and yellow,
With his long and glossy plumage,
Stood and beckoned at the doorway.
And as one in slumber walking,
Pale and haggard, but undaunted,
From the wigwam Hiawatha
Came and wrestled with Mondamin.

Round about him spun the landscape,
Sky and forest reeled together,
And his strong heart leaped within him,
As the sturgeon leaps and struggles
In a net to break its meshes.
Like a ring of fire around him
Blazed and flared the red horizon,
And a hundred suns seemed looking
At the combat of the wrestlers.

Suddenly upon the greensward
All alone stood Hiawatha,
Panting with his wild exertion,
Palpitating with the struggle;
And before him, breathless, lifeless,
Lay the youth, with hair dishevelled,

Plumage torn, and garments tattered,
Dead he lay there in the sunset.

    And victorious Hiawatha
Made the grave as he commanded,
Stripped the garments from Mondamin,
Stripped his tattered plumage from him,
Laid him in the earth, and made it
Soft and loose and light above him;
And the heron, the Shuh-shuh-gah,
From the melancholy moorlands,
Gave a cry of lamentation,
Gave a cry of pain and anguish!

    Homeward then went Hiawatha
To the lodge of old Nokomis,
And the seven days of his fasting
Were accomplished and completed.
But the place was not forgotten
Where he wrestled with Mondamin;
Nor forgotten nor neglected
Was the grave where lay Mondamin,
Sleeping in the rain and sunshine,
Where his scattered plumes and garments
Faded in the rain and sunshine.

    Day by day did Hiawatha

Go to wait and watch beside it;
Kept the dark mould soft above it,
Kept it clean from weeds and insects,
Drove away, with scoffs and shoutings,
Kahgahgee, the king of ravens.

Till at length a small green feather
From the earth shot slowly upward,
Then another and another,
And before the Summer ended
Stood the maize in all its beauty,
With its shining robes about it,
And its long, soft, yellow tresses;
And in rapture Hiawatha
Cried aloud:—"It is Mondamin!
Yes, the friend of man, Mondamin!"

Then he called to old Nokomis
And Iagoo, the great boaster,
Showed them where the maize was growing,
Told them of his wondrous vision,
Of his wrestling and his triumph,
Of this new gift to the nations,
Which should be their food for ever.

And still later, when the Autumn
Changed the long, green leaves to yellow,

And the soft and juicy kernels
Grew like wampum hard and yellow,
Then the ripened ears he gathered,
Stripped the withered husks from off them,
As he once had stripped the wrestler,
Gave the first Feast of Mondamin,
And made known unto the people
This new gift of the Great Spirit.

## VI.

### HIAWATHA'S FRIENDS.

Two good friends had Hiawatha,
Singled out from all the others,
Bound to him in closest union,
And to whom he gave the right hand
Of his heart, in joy and sorrow;
Chibiabos, the musician,
And the very strong man, Kwasind.

Straight between them ran the pathway,
Never grew the grass upon it;
Singing birds, that utter falsehoods,
Story-tellers, mischief-makers,
Found no eager ear to listen,
Could not breed ill-will between them,
For they kept each other's counsel,
Spake with naked hearts together,
Pondering much and much contriving

How the tribes of men might prosper.
    Most beloved by Hiawatha
Was the gentle Chibiabos,
He the best of all musicians,
He the sweetest of all singers.
Beautiful and childlike was he,
Brave as man is, soft as woman,
Pliant as a wand of willow,
Stately as a deer with antlers.

    When he sang, the village listened;
All the warriors gathered round him,
All the women came to hear him;
Now he stirred their souls to passion,
Now he melted them to pity.

    From the hollow reeds he fashioned
Flutes so musical and mellow,
That the brook, the Sebowisha,
Ceased to murmur in the woodland,
That the wood-birds ceased from singing,
And the squirrel, Adjidaumo,
Ceased his chatter in the oak-tree,
And the rabbit, the Wabasso,
Sat upright to look and listen.

    Yes, the brook, the Sebowisha,

Pausing, said: — "O Chibiabos,
Teach my waves to flow in music,
Softly as your words in singing!"

Yes, the blue-bird, the Owaissa,
Envious, said: — "O Chibiabos,
Teach me tones as wild and wayward,
Teach me songs as full of frenzy!"

Yes, the Opechee, the robin,
Joyous, said: — "O Chibiabos,
Teach me tones as sweet and tender,
Teach me songs as full of gladness!"

And the whippoorwill, Wawonaissa,
Sobbing, said: — "O Chibiabos,
Teach me tones as melancholy,
Teach me songs as full of sadness!"

All the many sounds of nature
Borrowed sweetness from his singing;
All the hearts of men were softened
By the pathos of his music;
For he sang of peace and freedom,
Sang of beauty, love, and longing;
Sang of death, and life undying
In the Islands of the Blessed,
In the kingdom of Ponemah,

In the land of the Hereafter.
    Very dear to Hiawatha
Was the gentle Chibiabos,
He the best of all musicians,
He the sweetest of all singers;
For his gentleness he loved him,
And the magic of his singing.
    Dear, too, unto Hiawatha
Was the very strong man, Kwasind,
He the strongest of all mortals,
He the mightiest among many;
For his very strength he loved him,
For his strength allied to goodness.
    Idle in his youth was Kwasind,
Very listless, dull, and dreamy,
Never played with other children,
Never fished and never hunted,
Not like other children was he;
But they saw that much he fasted,
Much his Manito entreated,
Much besought his Guardian Spirit.
    "Lazy Kwasind!" said his mother,
"In my work you never help me!
In the Summer you are roaming

Idly in the fields and forests;
In the Winter you are cowering
O'er the firebrands in the wigwam!
In the coldest days of Winter
I must break the ice for fishing;
With my nets you never help me!
At the door my nets are hanging,
Dripping, freezing with the water;
Go and wring them, Yenadizze!
Go and dry them in the sunshine!"

Slowly, from the ashes, Kwasind
Rose, but made no angry answer;
From the lodge went forth in silence,
Took the nets, that hung together,
Dripping, freezing at the doorway,
Like a wisp of straw he wrung them,
Like a wisp of straw he broke them,
Could not wring them without breaking,
Such the strength was in his fingers.

"Lazy Kwasind!" said his father,
"In the hunt you never help me;
Every bow you touch is broken,
Snapped asunder every arrow;
Yet come with me to the forest,

You shall bring the hunting homeward."
   Down a narrow pass they wandered,
Where a brooklet led them onward,
Where the trail of deer and bison
Marked the soft mud on the margin,
Till they found all further passage
Shut against them, barred securely
By the trunks of trees uprooted,
Lying lengthwise, lying crosswise,
And forbidding further passage.
   "We must go back," said the old man,
" O'er these logs we cannot clamber;
Not a woodchuck could get through them,
Not a squirrel clamber o'er them!"
And straightway his pipe he lighted,
And sat down to smoke and ponder.
But before his pipe was finished,
Lo! the path was cleared before him;
All the trunks had Kwasind lifted,
To the right hand, to the left hand,
Shot the pine-trees swift as arrows,
Hurled the cedars light as lances.
   "Lazy Kwasind!" said the young men,
As they sported in the meadow;

"Why stand idly looking at us,
Leaning on the rock behind you?
Come and wrestle with the others,
Let us pitch the quoit together!"

Lazy Kwasind made no answer,
To their challenge made no answer,
Only rose, and, slowly turning,
Seized the huge rock in his fingers,
Tore it from its deep foundation,
Poised it in the air a moment,
Pitched it sheer into the river,
Sheer into the swift Pauwating,
Where it still is seen in Summer.

Once as down that foaming river,
Down the rapids of Pauwating,
Kwasind sailed with his companions,
In the stream he saw a beaver,
Saw Ahmeek, the King of Beavers,
Struggling with the rushing currents,
Rising, sinking in the water.

Without speaking, without pausing,
Kwasind leaped into the river,
Plunged beneath the bubbling surface,
Through the whirlpools chased the beaver,

Followed him among the islands,
Stayed so long beneath the water,
That his terrified companions
Cried: "Alas! good bye to Kwasind!
We shall never more see Kwasind!"
But he reappeared triumphant,
And upon his shining shoulders
Brought the beaver, dead and dripping,
Brought the King of all the Beavers.

And these two, as I have told you,
Were the friends of Hiawatha,
Chibiabos, the musician,
And the very strong man, Kwasind.
Long they lived in peace together,
Spake with naked hearts together,
Pondering much and much contriving
How the tribes of men might prosper.

## VII.

### HIAWATHA'S SAILING.

"Give me of your bark, O Birch-Tree!
Of your yellow bark, O Birch-Tree!
Growing by the rushing river,
Tall and stately in the valley!
I a light canoe will build me,
Build a swift Cheemaun for sailing,
That shall float upon the river,
Like a yellow leaf in Autumn,
Like a yellow water-lily!

"Lay aside your cloak, O Birch-Tree!
Lay aside your white-skin wrapper,
For the Summer-time is coming,
And the sun is warm in heaven,
And you need no white-skin wrapper!"

Thus aloud cried Hiawatha
In the solitary forest,

By the rushing Taquamenaw,
When the birds were singing gayly,
In the Moon of Leaves were singing,
And the sun, from sleep awaking,
Started up and said, "Behold me!
Geezis, the great Sun, behold me!"

And the tree with all its branches
Rustled in the breeze of morning,
Saying, with a sigh of patience,
"Take my cloak, O Hiawatha!"

With his knife the tree he girdled;
Just beneath its lowest branches,
Just above the roots, he cut it,
Till the sap came oozing outward;
Down the trunk, from top to bottom,
Sheer he cleft the bark asunder,
With a wooden wedge he raised it,
Stripped it from the trunk unbroken.

"Give me of your boughs, O Cedar!
Of your strong and pliant branches,
My canoe to make more steady,
Make more strong and firm beneath me!"

Through the summit of the Cedar
Went a sound, a cry of horror,

Went a murmur of resistance;
But it whispered, bending downward,
"Take my boughs, O Hiawatha!"

Down he hewed the boughs of cedar,
Shaped them straightway to a framework,
Like two bows he formed and shaped them,
Like two bended bows together.

"Give me of your roots, O Tamarack!
Of your fibrous roots, O Larch-Tree!
My canoe to bind together,
So to bind the ends together
That the water may not enter,
That the river may not wet me!"

And the Larch, with all its fibres,
Shivered in the air of morning,
Touched his forehead with its tassels,
Said, with one long sigh of sorrow,
"Take them all, O Hiawatha!"

From the earth he tore the fibres,
Tore the tough roots of the Larch-Tree,
Closely sewed the bark together,
Bound it closely to the framework.

"Give me of your balm, O Fir-Tree!
Of your balsam and your resin,

So to close the seams together
That the water may not enter,
That the river may not wet me!"

And the Fir-Tree, tall and sombre,
Sobbed through all its robes of darkness,
Rattled like a shore with pebbles,
Answered wailing, answered weeping,
"Take my balm, O Hiawatha!"

And he took the tears of balsam,
Took the resin of the Fir-Tree,
Smeared therewith each seam and fissure,
Made each crevice safe from water.

"Give me of your quills, O Hedgehog!
All your quills, O Kagh, the Hedgehog!
I will make a necklace of them,
Make a girdle for my beauty,
And two stars to deck her bosom!"

From a hollow tree the Hedgehog
With his sleepy eyes looked at him,
Shot his shining quills, like arrows,
Saying, with a drowsy murmur,
Through the tangle of his whiskers,
"Take my quills, O Hiawatha!"

From the ground the quills he gathered,

All the little shining arrows,
Stained them red and blue and yellow,
With the juice of roots and berries;
Into his canoe he wrought them,
Round its waist a shining girdle,
Round its bows a gleaming necklace,
On its breast two stars resplendent.

Thus the Birch Canoe was builded
In the valley, by the river,
In the bosom of the forest;
And the forest's life was in it,
All its mystery and its magic,
All the lightness of the birch-tree,
All the toughness of the cedar,
All the larch's supple sinews;
And it floated on the river
Like a yellow leaf in Autumn,
Like a yellow water-lily.

Paddles none had Hiawatha,
Paddles none he had or needed,
For his thoughts as paddles served him,
And his wishes served to guide him;
Swift or slow at will he glided,
Veered to right or left at pleasure.

Then he called aloud to Kwasind,
To his friend, the strong man, Kwasind,
Saying: "Help me clear this river
Of its sunken logs and sand-bars."

Straight into the river Kwasind
Plunged as if he were an otter,
Dived as if he were a beaver,
Stood up to his waist in water,
To his arm-pits in the river,
Swam and shouted in the river,
Tugged at sunken logs and branches,
With his hands he scooped the sand-bars,
With his feet the ooze and tangle.

And thus sailed my Hiawatha
Down the rushing Taquamenaw,
Sailed through all its bends and windings,
Sailed through all its deeps and shallows,
While his friend, the strong man, Kwasind,
Swam the deeps, the shallows waded.

Up and down the river went they,
In and out among its islands,
Cleared its bed of root and sand-bar,
Dragged the dead trees from its channel,
Made its passage safe and certain,

Made a pathway for the people,
From its springs among the mountains,
To the waters of Pauwating,
To the bay of Taquamenaw,

## VIII.

### HIAWATHA'S FISHING.

FORTH upon the Gitche Gumee,
On the shining Big-Sea-Water,
With his fishing-line of cedar,
Of the twisted bark of cedar,
Forth to catch the sturgeon Nahma,
Mishe-Nahma, King of Fishes,
In his birch canoe exulting
All alone went Hiawatha.

Through the clear, transparent water
He could see the fishes swimming
Far down in the depths below him;
See the yellow perch, the Sahwa,
Like a sunbeam in the water,
See the Shawgashee, the craw-fish,
Like a spider on the bottom,
On the white and sandy bottom.

At the stern sat Hiawatha,
With his fishing-line of cedar;
In his plumes the breeze of morning
Played as in the hemlock branches;
On the bows, with tail erected,
Sat the squirrel, Adjidaumo;
In his fur the breeze of morning
Played as in the prairie grasses.

On the white sand of the bottom
Lay the monster Mishe-Nahma,
Lay the sturgeon, King of Fishes;
Through his gills he breathed the water,
With his fins he fanned and winnowed,
With his tail he swept the sand-floor.

There he lay in all his armor;
On each side a shield to guard him,
Plates of bone upon his forehead,
Down his sides and back and shoulders
Plates of bone with spines projecting!
Painted was he with his war-paints,
Stripes of yellow, red, and azure,
Spots of brown and spots of sable;
And he lay there on the bottom,
Fanning with his fins of purple,

As above him Hiawatha
In his birch canoe came sailing,
With his fishing-line of cedar.
   "Take my bait!" cried Hiawatha,
Down into the depths beneath him,
   "Take my bait, O Sturgeon, Nahma!
Come up from below the water,
Let us see which is the stronger!"
And he dropped his line of cedar
Through the clear, transparent water,
Waited vainly for an answer,
Long sat waiting for an answer,
And repeating loud and louder,
"Take my bait, O King of Fishes!"
   Quiet lay the sturgeon, Nahma,
Fanning slowly in the water,
Looking up at Hiawatha,
Listening to his call and clamor,
His unnecessary tumult,
Till he wearied of the shouting;
And he said to the Kenozha,
To the pike, the Maskenozha:
"Take the bait of this rude fellow,
Break the line of Hiawatha!"

In his fingers Hiawatha
Felt the loose line jerk and tighten;
As he drew it in, it tugged so
That the birch canoe stood endwise,
Like a birch log in the water,
With the squirrel, Adjidaumo,
Perched and frisking on the summit.

Full of scorn was Hiawatha
When he saw the fish rise upward,
Saw the pike, the Maskenozha,
Coming nearer, nearer to him,
And he shouted through the water:
"Esa! esa! Shame upon you!
You are but the pike, Kenozha,
You are not the fish I wanted,
You are not the King of Fishes!"

Reeling downward to the bottom
Sank the pike in great confusion,
And the mighty sturgeon, Nahma,
Said to Ugudwash, the sun-fish:
"Take the bait of this great boaster,
Break the line of Hiawatha!"

Slowly upward, wavering, gleaming
Like a white moon in the water,

Rose the Ugudwash, the sun-fish,
Seized the line of Hiawatha,
Swung with all his weight upon it,
Made a whirlpool in the water,
Whirled the birch canoe in circles,
Round and round in gurgling eddies,
Till the circles in the water
Reached the far-off sandy beaches,
Till the water-flags and rushes
Nodded on the distant margins.

But when Hiawatha saw him
Slowly rising through the water,
Litting his great disc of whiteness,
Loud he shouted in derision:
" Esa! esa! Shame upon you!
You are Ugudwash, the sun-fish,
You are not the fish I wanted,
You are not the King of Fishes!"

Wavering downward, white and ghastly,
Sank the Ugudwash, the sun-fish,
And again the sturgeon, Nahma,
Heard the shout of Hiawatha,
Heard his challenge of defiance,
The unnecessary tumult,

Ringing far across the water.

From the white sand of the bottom
Up he rose with angry gesture,
Quivering in each nerve and fibre,
Clashing all his plates of armor,
Gleaming bright with all his war-paint;
In his wrath he darted upward,
Flashing leaped into the sunshine,
Opened his great jaws, and swallowed
Both canoe and Hiawatha.

Down into that darksome cavern
Plunged the headlong Hiawatha,
As a log on some black river
Shoots and plunges down the rapids,
Found himself in utter darkness,
Groped about in helpless wonder,
Till he felt a great heart beating,
Throbbing in that utter darkness.

And he smote it in his anger,
With his fist, the heart of Nahma,
Felt the mighty King of Fishes
Shudder through each nerve and fibre,
Heard the water gurgle round him
As he leaped and staggered through it,

Sick at heart, and faint and weary.
  Crosswise then did Hiawatha
Drag his birch canoe for safety,
Lest from out the jaws of Nahma,
In the turmoil and confusion,
Forth he might be hurled and perish.
And the squirrel, Adjidaumo,
Frisked and chattered very gayly,
Toiled and tugged with Hiawatha
Till the labor was completed.
  Then said Hiawatha to him:
"O my little friend, the squirrel,
Bravely have you toiled to help me;
Take the thanks of Hiawatha,
And the name which now he gives you;
For hereafter and for ever
Boys shall call you Adjidaumo,
Tail-in-air the boys shall call you!"
  And again the sturgeon, Nahma,
Gasped and quivered in the water,
Then was still, and drifted landward
Till he grated on the pebbles,
Till the listening Hiawatha
Heard him grate upon the margin,

Felt him strand upon the pebbles,
Knew that Nahma, King of Fishes,
Lay there dead upon the margin.

Then he heard a clang and flapping,
As of many wings assembling,
Heard a screaming and confusion,
As of birds of prey contending,
Saw a gleam of light above him,
Shining through the ribs of Nahma,
Saw the glittering eyes of sea-gulls,
Of Kayoshk, the sea-gulls, peering,
Gazing at him through the opening,
Heard them saying to each other,
"'T is our brother, Hiawatha!"

And he shouted from below them,
Cried exulting from the caverns:
"O ye sea-gulls! O my brothers!
I have slain the sturgeon, Nahma;
Make the rifts a little larger,
With your claws the openings widen,
Set me free from this dark prison,
And henceforward and for ever
Men shall speak of your achievements,
Calling you Kayoshk, the sea-gulls,

Yes, Kayoshk, the Noble Scratchers!"
　　And the wild and clamorous sea-gulls
Toiled with beak and claws together,
Made the rifts and openings wider
In the mighty ribs of Nahma,
And from peril and from prison,
From the body of the sturgeon,
From the peril of the water,
Was released my Hiawatha.

　　He was standing near his wigwam,
On the margin of the water,
And he called to old Nokomis,
Called and beckoned to Nokomis,
Pointed to the sturgeon, Nahma,
Lying lifeless on the pebbles,
With the sea-gulls feeding on him.

　　"I have slain the Mishe-Nahma,
Slain the King of Fishes!" said he;
"Look! the sea-gulls feed upon him,
Yes, my friend Kayoshk, the sea-gulls;
Drive them not away, Nokomis,
They have saved me from great peril
In the body of the sturgeon,
Wait until their meal is ended,

Till their craws are full with feasting,
Till they homeward fly, at sunset,
To their nests among the marshes;
Then bring all your pots and kettles,
And make oil for us in Winter."

And she waited till the sun set,
Till the pallid moon, the night-sun,
Rose above the tranquil water,
Till Kayoshk, the sated sea-gulls,
From their banquet rose with clamor,
And across the fiery sunset
Winged their way to far-off islands,
To their nests among the rushes.

To his sleep went Hiawatha,
And Nokomis to her labor,
Toiling patient in the moonlight,
Till the sun and moon changed places,
Till the sky was red with sunrise,
And Kayoshk, the hungry sea-gulls,
Came back from the reedy islands,
Clamorous for their morning banquet.

Three whole days and nights alternate
Old Nokomis and the sea-gulls
Stripped the oily flesh of Nahma,

Till the waves washed through the rib-bones,
Till the sea-gulls came no longer,
And upon the sands lay nothing
But the skeleton of Nahma.

## IX.

### HIAWATHA AND THE PEARL-FEATHER.

On the shores of Gitche Gumee,
Of the shining Big-Sea-Water
Stood Nokomis, the old woman,
Pointing with her finger westward,
O'er the water pointing westward,
To the purple clouds of sunset.

Fiercely the red sun descending
Burned his way along the heavens,
Set the sky on fire behind him,
As war-parties, when retreating,
Burn the prairies on their war-trail;
And the moon, the night-sun, eastward,
Suddenly starting from his ambush,
Followed fast those bloody footprints,
Followed in that fiery war-trail,
With its glare upon his features.

And Nokomis, the old woman,
Pointing with her finger westward,
Spake these words to Hiawatha:
"Yonder dwells the great Pearl-Feather,
Megissogwon, the Magician,
Manito of Wealth and Wampum,
Guarded by his fiery serpents,
Guarded by the black pitch-water.
You can see his fiery serpents,
The Kenabeek, the great serpents,
Coiling, playing in the water;
You can see the black pitch-water
Stretching far away beyond them,
To the purple clouds of sunset!

"He it was who slew my father,
By his wicked wiles and cunning,
When he from the moon descended,
When he came on earth to seek me.
He, the mightiest of Magicians,
Sends the fever from the marshes,
Sends the pestilential vapors,
Sends the poisonous exhalations,
Sends the white fog from the fen-lands,
Sends disease and death among us!

"Take your bow, O Hiawatha,
Take your arrows, jasper-headed,
Take your war-club, Puggawaugun,
And your mittens, Minjekahwun,
And your birch-canoe for sailing,
And the oil of Mishe-Nahma,
So to smear its sides, that swiftly
You may pass the black pitch-water;
Slay this merciless magician,
Save the people from the fever
That he breathes across the fen-lands,
And avenge my father's murder!"

Straightway then my Hiawatha
Armed himself with all his war-gear,
Launched his birch-canoe for sailing;
With his palm its sides he patted,
Said with glee: "Cheemaun, my darling,
O my Birch-Canoe! leap forward,
Where you see the fiery serpents,
Where you see the black pitch-water!"

Forward leaped Cheemaun exulting,
And the noble Hiawatha
Sang his war-song wild and woful,
And above him the war-eagle,

The Keneu, the great war-eagle,
Master of all fowls with feathers,
Screamed and hurtled through the heavens
  Soon he reached the fiery serpents,
The Kenabeek, the great serpents,
Lying huge upon the water,
Sparkling, rippling in the water,
Lying coiled across the passage,
With their blazing crests uplifted,
Breathing fiery fogs and vapors,
So that none could pass beyond them.
  But the fearless Hiawatha
Cried aloud, and spake in this wise:
"Let me pass my way, Kenabeek,
Let me go upon my journey!"
And they answered, hissing fiercely,
With their fiery breath made answer:
"Back, go back! O Shaugodaya!
Back to old Nokomis, Faint-heart!"
  Then the angry Hiawatha
Raised his mighty bow of ash-tree,
Seized his arrows, jasper-headed,
Shot them fast among the serpents;
Every twanging of the bow-string

Was a war-cry and a death-cry,
Every whizzing of an arrow
Was a death-song of Kenabeek.

Weltering in the bloody water,
Dead lay all the fiery serpents,
And among them Hiawatha
Harmless sailed, and cried exulting:
"Onward, O Cheemaun, my darling!
Onward to the black pitch-water!"

Then he took the oil of Nahma,
And the bows and sides anointed,
Smeared them well with oil, that swiftly
He might pass the black pitch-water.

All night long he sailed upon it,
Sailed upon that sluggish water,
Covered with its mould of ages,
Black with rotting water-rushes,
Rank with flags and leaves of lilies,
Stagnant, lifeless, dreary, dismal,
Lighted by the shimmering moonlight,
And by will-o'-the-wisps illumined,
Fires by ghosts of dead men kindled,
In their weary night encampments.

All the air was white with moonlight,

All the water black with shadow,
And around him the Suggema,
The mosquitos, sang their war-song,
And the fire-flies, Wah-wah-taysee,
Waved their torches to mislead him;
And the bull-frog, the Dahinda,
Thrust his head into the moonlight,
Fixed his yellow eyes upon him,
Sobbed and sank beneath the surface;
And anon a thousand whistles,
Answered over all the fen-lands,
And the heron, the Shuh-shuh-gah,
Far off on the reedy margin,
Heralded the hero's coming.

Westward thus fared Hiawatha,
Toward the realm of Megissogwon,
Toward the land of the Pearl-Feather,
Till the level moon stared at him,
In his face stared pale and haggard,
Till the sun was hot behind him,
Till it burned upon his shoulders,
And before him on the upland
He could see the Shining Wigwam
Of the Manito of Wampum,

Of the mightiest of Magicians.

Then once more Cheemaun he patted,
To his birch-canoe said, "Onward!"
And it stirred in all its fibres,
And with one great bound of triumph
Leaped across the water-lilies,
Leaped through tangled flags and rushes,
And upon the beach beyond them
Dry-shod landed Hiawatha.

Straight he took his bow of ash-tree,
One end on the sand he rested,
With his knee he pressed the middle,
Stretched the faithful bow-string tighter,
Took an arrow, jasper-headed,
Shot it at the Shining Wigwam,
Sent it singing as a herald,
As a bearer of his message,
Of his challenge loud and lofty:
"Come forth from your lodge, Pearl-Feather!
Hiawatha waits your coming!"

Straightway from the Shining Wigwam
Came the mighty Megissogwon,
Tall of stature, broad of shoulder,
Dark and terrible in aspect,

Clad from head to foot in wampum,
Armed with all his warlike weapons,
Painted like the sky of morning,
Streaked with crimson, blue and yellow,
Crested with great eagle-feathers,
Streaming upward, streaming outward.

"Well I know you, Hiawatha!"
Cried he in a voice of thunder,
In a tone of loud derision.
"Hasten back, O Shaugodaya!
Hasten back among the women,
Back to old Nokomis, Faint-heart!
I will slay you as you stand there,
As of old I slew her father!"

But my Hiawatha answered,
Nothing daunted, fearing nothing:
"Big words do not smite like war-clubs,
Boastful breath is not a bow-string,
Taunts are not so sharp as arrows,
Deeds are better things than words are,
Actions mightier than boastings!"

Then began the greatest battle
That the sun had ever looked on,
That the war-birds ever witnessed.

All a Summer's day it lasted,
From the sunrise to the sunset;
For the shafts of Hiawatha
Harmless hit the shirt of wampum,
Harmless fell the blows he dealt it
With his mittens, Minjekahwun,
Harmless fell the heavy war-club;
It could dash the rocks asunder,
But it could not break the meshes
Of that magic shirt of wampum.

Till at sunset Hiawatha,
Leaning on his bow of ash-tree,
Wounded, weary, and desponding,
With his mighty war-club broken,
With his mittens torn and tattered,
And three useless arrows only,
Paused to rest beneath a pine-tree,
From whose branches trailed the mosses,
And whose trunk was coated over
With the Dead-man's Moccasin-leather,
With the fungus white and yellow.

Suddenly from the boughs above him
Sang the Mama, the woodpecker:
"Aim your arrows, Hiawatha,

At the head of Megissogwon,
Strike the tuft of hair upon it,
At their roots the long black tresses;
There alone can he be wounded!"

Winged with feathers, tipped with jasper,
Swift flew Hiawatha's arrow,
Just as Megissogwon, stooping,
Raised a heavy stone to throw it.
Full upon the crown it struck him,
At the roots of his long tresses,
And he reeled and staggered forward,
Plunging like a wounded bison,
Yes, like Pezhekee, the bison,
When the snow is on the prairie.

Swifter flew the second arrow,
In the pathway of the other,
Piercing deeper than the other,
Wounding sorer than the other;
And the knees of Megissogwon
Shook like windy reeds beneath **him,**
Bent and trembled like the rushes.

But the third and latest arrow
Swiftest flew, and wounded sorest,
And the mighty Megissogwon

Saw the fiery eyes of Pauguk,
Saw the eyes of Death glare at him,
Heard his voice call in the darkness;
At the feet of Hiawatha
Lifeless lay the great Pearl-Feather,
Lay the mightiest of Magicians.

Then the grateful Hiawatha
Called the Mama, the woodpecker,
From his perch among the branches
Of the melancholy pine-tree,
And, in honor of his service,
Stained with blood the tuft of feathers
On the little head of Mama;
Even to this day he wears it,
Wears the tuft of crimson feathers,
As a symbol of his service.

Then he stripped the shirt of wampum
From the back of Megissogwon,
As a trophy of the battle,
As a signal of his conquest.
On the shore he left the body,
Half on land and half in water,
In the sand his feet were buried,
And his face was in the water.

And above him, wheeled and clamored
The Keneu, the great war-eagle,
Sailing round in narrower circles,
Hovering nearer, nearer, nearer.

From the wigwam Hiawatha
Bore the wealth of Megissogwon,
All his wealth of skins and wampum,
Furs of bison and of beaver,
Furs of sable and of ermine,
Wampum belts and strings and pouches,
Quivers wrought with beads of wampum,
Filled with arrows, silver-headed.

Homeward then he sailed exulting,
Homeward through the black pitch-water,
Homeward through the weltering serpents,
With the trophies of the battle,
With a shout and song of triumph.

On the shore stood old Nokomis,
On the shore stood Chibiabos,
And the very strong man, Kwasind,
Waiting for the hero's coming,
Listening to his song of triumph.
And the people of the village
Welcomed him with songs and dances,

Made a joyous feast, and shouted:
"Honor be to Hiawatha!
He has slain the great Pearl-Feather,
Slain the mightiest of Magicians,
Him, who sent the fiery fever,
Sent the white fog from the fen-lands,
Sent disease and death among us!"
  Ever dear to Hiawatha
Was the memory of Mama!
And in token of his friendship,
As a mark of his remembrance,
He adorned and decked his pipe-stem
With the crimson tuft of feathers,
With the blood-red crest of Mama.
But the wealth of Megissogwon,
All the trophies of the battle,
He divided with his people,
Shared it equally among them.

## X.

#### HIAWATHA'S WOOING.

"As unto the bow the cord is,
So unto the man is woman,
Though she bends him, she obeys him,
Though she draws him, yet she follows,
Useless each without the other!"

Thus the youthful Hiawatha
Said within himself and pondered,
Much perplexed by various feelings,
Listless, longing, hoping, fearing,
Dreaming still of Minnehaha,
Of the lovely Laughing Water,
In the land of the Dacotahs.

"Wed a maiden of your people,"
Warning said the old Nokomis;
"Go not eastward, go not westward,
For a stranger, whom we know not!

Like a fire upon the hearth-stone
Is a neighbor's homely daughter,
Like the starlight or the moonlight
Is the handsomest of strangers!"

Thus dissuading spake Nokomis,
And my Hiawatha answered
Only this: "Dear old Nokomis,
Very pleasant is the firelight,
But I like the starlight better,
Better do I like the moonlight!"

Gravely then said old Nokomis:
"Bring not here an idle maiden,
Bring not here a useless woman,
Hands unskilful, feet unwilling;
Bring a wife with nimble fingers,
Heart and hand that move together,
Feet that run on willing errands!"

Smiling answered Hiawatha:
"In the land of the Dacotahs
Lives the Arrow-maker's daughter,
Minnehaha, Laughing Water,
Handsomest of all the women.
I will bring her to your wigwam,
She shall run upon your errands,

Be your starlight, moonlight, firelight,
Be the sunlight of my people!"

Still dissuading said Nokomis:
"Bring not to my lodge a stranger
From the land of the Dacotahs!
Very fierce are the Dacotahs,
Often is there war between us,
There are feuds yet unforgotten,
Wounds that ache and still may open!"

Laughing answered Hiawatha:
"For that reason, if no other,
Would I wed the fair Dacotah,
That our tribes might be united,
That old feuds might be forgotten,
And old wounds be healed for ever!"

Thus departed Hiawatha
To the land of the Dacotahs,
To the land of handsome women;
Striding over moor and meadow,
Through interminable forests,
Through uninterrupted silence.

With his moccasins of magic,
At each stride a mile he measured;
Yet the way seemed long before him,

And his heart outrun his footsteps;
And he journeyed without resting,
Till he heard the cataract's thunder,
Heard the Falls of Minnehaha
Calling to him through the silence.
"Pleasant is the sound!" he murmured,
"Pleasant is the voice that calls me!"

On the outskirts of the forest,
'Twixt the shadow and the sunshine,
Herds of fallow deer were feeding,
But they saw not Hiawatha;
To his bow he whispered, "Fail not!"
To his arrow whispered, "Swerve not!"
Sent it singing on its errand,
To the red heart of the roebuck;
Threw the deer across his shoulder,
And sped forward without pausing.

At the doorway of his wigwam
Sat the ancient Arrow-maker,
In the land of the Dacotahs,
Making arrow-heads of jasper,
Arrow-heads of chalcedony.
At his side, in all her beauty,
Sat the lovely Minnehaha,

Sat his daughter, Laughing Water,
Plaiting mats of flags and rushes;
Of the past the old man's thoughts were,
And the maiden's of the future.

He was thinking, as he sat there,
Of the days when with such arrows
He had struck the deer and bison,
On the Muskoday, the meadow;
Shot the wild goose, flying southward,
On the wing, the clamorous Wawa;
Thinking of the great war-parties,
How they came to buy his arrows,
Could not fight without his arrows.
Ah, no more such noble warriors
Could be found on earth as they were!
Now the men were all like women,
Only used their tongues for weapons!

She was thinking of a hunter,
From another tribe and country,
Young and tall and very handsome,
Who one morning, in the Spring-time,
Came to buy her father's arrows,
Sat and rested in the wigwam,
Lingered long about the doorway,

Looking back as he departed.
She had heard her father praise him,
Praise his courage and his wisdom;
Would he come again for arrows
To the Falls of Minnehaha?
On the mat her hands lay idle,
And her eyes were very dreamy.

Through their thoughts they heard a footstep,
Heard a rustling in the branches,
And with glowing cheek and forehead,
With the deer upon his shoulders,
Suddenly from out the woodlands
Hiawatha stood before them.

Straight the ancient Arrow-maker
Looked up gravely from his labor,
Laid aside the unfinished arrow,
Bade him enter at the doorway,
Saying, as he rose to meet him:
"Hiawatha, you are welcome!"

At the feet of Laughing Water
Hiawatha laid his burden,
Threw the red deer from his shoulders;
And the maiden looked up at him,
Looked up from her mat of rushes,

Said with gentle look and accent:
"You are welcome, Hiawatha!"

Very spacious was the wigwam,
Made of deer-skin dressed and whitened,
With the Gods of the Dacotahs
Drawn and painted on its curtains,
And so tall the doorway, hardly
Hiawatha stooped to enter,
Hardly touched his eagle-feathers
As he entered at the doorway.

Then uprose the Laughing Water,
From the ground fair Minnehaha,
Laid aside her mat unfinished,
Brought forth food and set before them,
Water brought them from the brooklet,
Gave them food in earthen vessels,
Gave them drink in bowls of bass-wood,
Listened while the guest was speaking,
Listened while her father answered,
But not once her lips she opened,
Not a single word she uttered.

Yes, as in a dream she listened
To the words of Hiawatha,
As he talked of old Nokomis,

Who had nursed him in his childhood,
As he told of his companions,
Chibiabos, the musician,
And the very strong man, Kwasind,
And of happiness and plenty
In the land of the Ojibways,
In the pleasant land and peaceful.

  "After many years of warfare,
Many years of strife and bloodshed,
There is peace between the Ojibways
And the tribe of the Dacotahs."
Thus continued Hiawatha,
And then added, speaking slowly:
"That this peace may last for ever,
And our hands be clasped more closely,
And our hearts be more united,
Give me as my wife this maiden,
Minnehaha, Laughing Water,
Loveliest of Dacotah women!"

  And the ancient Arrow-maker
Paused a moment ere he answered,
Smoked a little while in silence,
Looked at Hiawatha proudly,
Fondly looked at Laughing Water,

And made answer very gravely:
" Yes, if Minnehaha wishes;
Let your heart speak, Minnehaha!"
    And the lovely Laughing Water
Seemed more lovely, as she stood there,
Neither willing nor reluctant,
As she went to Hiawatha,
Softly took the seat beside him,
While she said, and blushed to say it,
"I will follow you, my husband!"
    This was Hiawatha's wooing!
Thus it was he won the daughter
Of the ancient Arrow-maker,
In the land of the Dacotahs!
    From the wigwam he departed,
Leading with him Laughing Water;
Hand in hand they went together,
Through the woodland and the meadow,
Left the old man standing lonely
At the doorway of his wigwam,
Heard the Falls of Minnehaha
Calling to them from the distance,
Crying to them from afar off:
"Fare thee well, O Minnehaha!"

And the ancient Arrow-maker
Turned again unto his labor,
Sat down by his sunny doorway,
Murmuring to himself, and saying:
"Thus it is our daughters leave us,
Those we love, and those who love us!
Just when they have learned to help us,
When we are old and lean upon them,
Comes a youth with flaunting feathers,
With his flute of reeds, a stranger
Wanders piping through the village,
Beckons to the fairest maiden,
And she follows where he leads her,
Leaving all things for the stranger!"

Pleasant was the journey homeward,
Through interminable forests,
Over meadow, over mountain,
Over river, hill, and hollow.
Short it seemed to Hiawatha,
Though they journeyed very slowly,
Though his pace he checked and slackened
To the steps of Laughing Water.
Over wide and rushing rivers

In his arms he bore the maiden;
Light he thought her as a feather,
As the plume upon his head-gear;
Cleared the tangled pathway for her,
Bent aside the swaying branches,
Made at night a lodge of branches,
And a bed with boughs of hemlock,
And a fire before the doorway
With the dry cones of the pine-tree.

All the travelling winds went with them,
O'er the meadow, through the forest;
All the stars of night looked at them,
Watched with sleepless eyes their slumber;
From his ambush in the oak-tree
Peeped the squirrel, Adjidaumo,
Watched with eager eyes the lovers;
And the rabbit, the Wabasso,
Scampered from the path before them,
Peering, peeping from his burrow,
Sat erect upon his haunches,
Watched with curious eyes the lovers.

Pleasant was the journey homeward!
All the birds sang loud and sweetly
Songs of happiness and heart's-ease:

Sang the blue-bird, the Owaissa:
"Happy are you, Hiawatha,
Having such a wife to love you!"
Sang the Opechee, the robin:
"Happy are you, Laughing Water,
Having such a noble husband!"

From the sky the sun benignant
Looked upon them through the branches,
Saying to them, "O my children,
Love is sunshine, hate is shadow,
Life is checkered shade and sunshine,
Rule by love, O Hiawatha!"

From the sky the moon looked at them,
Filled the lodge with mystic splendors,
Whispered to them: "O my children,
Day is restless, night is quiet,
Man imperious, woman feeble;
Half is mine, although I follow;
Rule by patience, Laughing Water!"

Thus it was they journeyed homeward;
Thus it was that Hiawatha,
To the lodge of old Nokomis
Brought the moonlight, starlight, firelight,
Brought the sunshine of his people,

Minnehaha, Laughing Water,
Handsomest of all the women
In the land of the Dacotahs,
In the land of handsome women.

## XI.

### HIAWATHA'S WEDDING—FEAST.

You shall hear how Pau-Puk-Keewis,
How the handsome Yenadizze
Danced at Hiawatha's wedding;
How the gentle Chibiabos,
He the sweetest of musicians,
Sang his songs of love and longing;
How Iagoo, the great boaster,
He the marvellous story-teller,
Told his tales of strange adventure,
That the feast might be more joyous,
That the time might pass more gayly,
And the guests be more contented.

Sumptuous was the feast Nokomis
Made at Hiawatha's wedding;
All the bowls were made of bass-wood,
White and polished very smoothly,

All the spoons of horn of bison,
Black and polished very smoothly.

She had sent through all the village
Messengers with wands of willow,
As a sign of invitation,
As a token of the feasting;
And the wedding guests assembled,
Clad in all their richest raiment,
Robes of fur and belts of wampum,
Splendid with their paint and plumage,
Beautiful with beads and tassels.

First they ate the sturgeon, Nahma,
And the pike, the Maskenozha,
Caught and cooked by old Nokomis;
Then on pemican they feasted,
Pemican and buffalo marrow,
Haunch of deer and hump of bison,
Yellow cakes of the Mondamin,
And the wild rice of the river.

But the gracious Hiawatha,
And the lovely Laughing Water,
And the careful old Nokomis,
Tasted not the food before them,
Only waited on the others,

Only served their guests in silence.
　　　And when all the guests had finished,
Old Nokomis, brisk and busy,
From an ample pouch of otter,
Filled the red stone pipes for smoking
With tobacco from the South-land,
Mixed with bark of the red willow,
And with herbs and leaves of fragrance.

Then she said: "O Pau-Puk-Keewis,
Dance for us your merry dances,
Dance the Beggar's Dance to please us,
That the feast may be more joyous,
That the time may pass more gayly,
And our guests be more contented!"

Then the handsome Pau-Puk-Keewis,
He the idle Yenadizze,
He the merry mischief-maker,
Whom the people called the Storm-Fool,
Rose among the guests assembled.

Skilled was he in sports and pastimes,
In the merry dance of snow-shoes,
In the play of quoits and ball-play;
Skilled was he in games of hazard,
In all games of skill and hazard,

Pugasaing, the Bowl and Counters,
Kuntassoo, the Game of Plum-stones.

Though the warriors called him Faint-Heart,
Called him coward, Shaugodaya,
Idler, gambler, Yenadizze,
Little heeded he their jesting,
Little cared he for their insults,
For the women and the maidens
Loved the handsome Pau-Puk-Keewis.

He was dressed in shirt of doe-skin,
White and soft, and fringed with ermine,
All inwrought with beads of wampum;
He was dressed in deer-skin leggings,
Fringed with hedgehog quills and ermine,
And in moccasins of buckskin,
Thick with quills and beads embroidered.
On his head were plumes of swan's down,
On his heels were tails of foxes,
In one hand a fan of feathers,
And a pipe was in the other.

Barred with streaks of red and yellow,
Streaks of blue and bright vermilion,
Shone the face of Pau-Puk-Keewis.
From his forehead fell his tresses,

Smooth, and parted like a woman's,
Shining bright with oil, and plaited,
Hung with braids of scented grasses,
As among the guests assembled,
To the sound of flutes and singing,
To the sound of drums and voices,
Rose the handsome Pau-Puk-Keewis,
And began his mystic dances.

First he danced a solemn measure,
Very slow in step and gesture,
In and out among the pine-trees,
Through the shadows and the sunshine,
Treading softly like a panther.
Then more swiftly and still swifter,
Whirling, spinning round in circles,
Leaping o'er the guests assembled,
Eddying round and round the wigwam,
Till the leaves went whirling with him,
Till the dust and wind together
Swept in eddies round about him.

Then along the sandy margin
Of the lake, the Big-Sea-Water,
On he sped with frenzied gestures,
Stamped upon the sand, and tossed it

Wildly in the air around him;
Till the wind became a whirlwind,
Till the sand was blown and sifted
Like great snowdrifts o'er the landscape,
Heaping all the shores with Sand Dunes,
Sand Hills of the Nagow Wudjoo!

Thus the merry Pau-Puk-Keewis
Danced his Beggar's Dance to please them,
And, returning, sat down laughing
There among the guests assembled,
Sat and fanned himself serenely
With his fan of turkey-feathers.

Then they said to Chibiabos,
To the friend of Hiawatha,
To the sweetest of all singers,
To the best of all musicians:—
"Sing to us, O Chibiabos!
Songs of love and songs of longing,
That the feast may be more joyous,
That the time may pass more gayly,
And our guests be more contented!"

And the gentle Chibiabos
Sang in accents sweet and tender,
Sang in tones of deep emotion,

Songs of love and songs of longing;
Looking still at Hiawatha,
Looking at fair Laughing Water,
Sang he softly, sang in this wise:

"Onaway! Awake, beloved!
Thou the wild-flower of the forest!
Thou the wild-bird of the prairie!
Thou with eyes so soft and fawn-like!

"If thou only lookest at me,
I am happy, I am happy,
As the lilies of the prairie,
When they feel the dew upon them!

"Sweet thy breath is as the fragrance
Of the wild-flowers in the morning,
As their fragrance is at evening,
In the Moon when leaves are falling.

"Does not all the blood within me
Leap to meet thee, leap to meet thee,
As the springs to meet the sunshine,
In the Moon when nights are brightest?

"Onaway! my heart sings to thee,
Sings with joy when thou art near me,
As the sighing, singing branches
In the pleasant Moon of Strawberries!

"When thou art not pleased, belovéd,
Then my heart is sad and darkened,
As the shining river darkens
When the clouds drop shadows on it!

"When thou smilest, my belovéd,
Then my troubled heart is brightened,
As in sunshine gleam the ripples
That the cold wind makes in rivers.

"Smiles the earth, and smile the waters,
Smile the cloudless skies above us,
But I lose the way of smiling
When thou art no longer near me!

"I myself, myself! behold me!
Blood of my beating heart behold me!
O awake, awake, belovéd!
Onaway! awake, belovéd!"

Thus the gentle Chibiabos
Sang his song of love and longing;
And Iagoo, the great boaster,
He the marvellous story-teller,
He the friend of old Nokomis,
Jealous of the sweet musician,
Jealous of the applause they gave him,
Saw in all the eyes around him,

Saw in all their looks and gestures,
That the wedding guests assembled
Longed to hear his pleasant stories,
His immeasurable falsehoods.

Very boastful was Iagoo;
Never heard he an adventure
But himself had met a greater;
Never any deed of daring
But himself had done a bolder;
Never any marvellous story
But himself could tell a stranger.

Would you listen to his boasting,
Would you only give him credence,
No one ever shot an arrow
Half so far and high as he had;
Ever caught so many fishes,
Ever killed so many reindeer,
Ever trapped so many beaver!

None could run so fast as he could,
None could dive so deep as he could,
None could swim so far as he could;
None had made so many journeys,
None had seen so many wonders,
As this wonderful Iagoo,

As this marvellous story-teller!
    Thus his name became a by-word
And a jest among the people;
And whene'er a boastful hunter
Praised his own address too highly,
Or a warrior, home returning,
Talked too much of his achievements,
All his hearers cried: "Iagoo!
Here's Iagoo come among us!"

    He it was who carved the cradle
Of the little Hiawatha,
Carved its framework out of linden,
Bound it strong with reindeer sinews;
He it was who taught him later
How to make his bows and arrows,
How to make the bows of ash-tree,
And the arrows of the oak-tree.
So among the guests assembled
At my Hiawatha's wedding
Sat Iagoo, old and ugly,
Sat the marvellous story-teller.

    And they said: "O good Iagoo,
Tell us now a tale of wonder,
Tell us of some strange adventure,

That the feast may be more joyous,
That the time may pass more gayly,
And our guests be more contented!"
    And Iagoo answered straightway:
"You shall hear a tale of wonder,
You shall hear the strange adventures
Of Osseo, the Magician,
From the Evening Star descended."

## XII.

### THE SON OF THE EVENING STAR.

CAN it be the sun descending
O'er the level plain of water?
Or the Red Swan floating, flying,
Wounded by the magic arrow,
Staining all the waves with crimson,
With the crimson of its life-blood,
Filling all the air with splendor,
With the splendor of its plumage?

Yes; it is the sun descending,
Sinking down into the water;
All the sky is stained with purple,
All the water flushed with crimson!
No; it is the Red Swan floating,
Diving down beneath the water;
To the sky its wings are lifted,
With its blood the waves are reddened!

Over it the Star of Evening
Melts and trembles through the purple,
Hangs suspended in the twilight.
No; it is a bead of wampum
On the róbes of the Great Spirit,
As he passes through the twilight,
Walks in silence through the heavens!

This with joy beheld Iagoo
And he said in haste: "Behold it!
See the sacred Star of Evening!
You shall hear a tale of wonder,
Hear the story of Osseo,
Son of the Evening Star, Osseo!

"Once, in days no more remembered,
Ages nearer the beginning,
When the heavens were closer to us,
And the Gods were more familiar,
In the North-land lived a hunter,
With ten young and comely daughters,
Tall and lithe as wands of willow;
Only Oweenee, the youngest,
She the wilful and the wayward,
She the silent, dreamy maiden,
Was the fairest of the sisters.

"All these women married warriors,
Married brave and haughty husbands;
Only Oweenee, the youngest,
Laughed and flouted all her lovers,
All her young and handsome suitors,
And then married old Osseo,
Old Osseo, poor and ugly,
Broken with age and weak with coughing,
Always coughing like a squirrel.

"Ah, but beautiful within him
Was the spirit of Osseo,
From the Evening Star descended,
Star of Evening, Star of Woman,
Star of tenderness and passion!
All its fire was in his bosom
All its beauty in his spirit,
All its mystery in his being,
All its splendor in his language!

"And her lovers, the rejected,
Handsome men with belts of wampum,
Handsome men with paint and feathers,
Pointed at her in derision,
Followed her with jest and laughter.
But she said: 'I care not for you,

Care not for your belts of wampum,
Care not for your paint and feathers,
Care not for your jests and laughter;
I am happy with Osseo!'

"Once to some great feast invited,
Through the damp and dusk of evening
Walked together the ten sisters,
Walked together with their husbands;
Slowly followed old Osseo,
With fair Oweenee beside him;
All the others chatted gayly,
These two only walked in silence.

"At the western sky Osseo
Gazed intent, as if imploring,
Often stopped and gazed imploring
At the trembling Star of Evening,
At the tender Star of Woman;
And they heard him murmur softly:
'*Ah, showain nemeshin, Nosa!*
Pity, pity me, my father!'

"'Listen!' said the eldest sister,
'He is praying to his father!
What a pity that the old man
Does not stumble in the pathway,

Does not break his neck by falling!'
And they laughed till all the forest
Rang with their unseemly laughter.

"On their pathway through the woodlands
Lay an oak, by storms uprooted,
Lay the great trunk of an oak-tree,
Buried half in leaves and mosses,
Mouldering, crumbling, huge and hollow.
And Osseo, when he saw it,
Gave a shout, a cry of anguish,
Leaped into its yawning cavern,
At one end went in an old man,
Wasted, wrinkled, old, and ugly;
From the other came a young man,
Tall and straight and strong and handsome.

"Thus Osseo was transfigured,
Thus restored to youth and beauty;
But, alas for good Osseo,
And for Oweenee, the faithful!
Strangely, too, was she transfigured.
Changed into a weak old woman,
With a staff she tottered onward,
Wasted, wrinkled, old, and ugly!
And the sisters and their husbands

Laughed until the echoing forest
Rang with their unseemly laughter.

"But Osseo turned not from her,
Walked with slower step beside her,
Took her hand, as brown and withered
As an oak-leaf is in Winter,
Called her sweetheart, Nenemoosha,
Soothed her with soft words of kindness,
Till they reached the lodge of feasting,
Till they sat down in the wigwam,
Sacred to the Star of Evening,
To the tender Star of Woman.

"Wrapt in visions, lost in dreaming,
At the banquet sat Osseo;
All were merry, all were happy,
All were joyous but Osseo.
Neither food nor drink he tasted,
Neither did he speak nor listen,
But as one bewildered sat he,
Looking dreamily and sadly,
First at Oweenee, then upward
At the gleaming sky above them.

"Then a voice was heard, a whisper,
Coming from the starry distance,

Coming from the empty vastness,
Low, and musical, and tender;
And the voice said: 'O Osseo!
O my son, my best beloved!
Broken are the spells that bound you,
All the charms of the magicians,
All the magic powers of evil;
Come to me; ascend, Osseo!

"'Taste the food that stands before you:
It is blessed and enchanted,
It has magic virtues in it,
It will change you to a spirit.
All your bowls and all your kettles
Shall be wood and clay no longer;
But the bowls be changed to wampum,
And the kettles shall be silver;
They shall shine like shells of scarlet,
Like the fire shall gleam and glimmer.

"'And the women shall no longer
Bear the dreary doom of labor,
But be changed to birds, and glisten
With the beauty of the starlight,
Painted with the dusky splendors
Of the skies and clouds of evening!'

'What Osseo heard as whispers,
What as words he comprehended,
Was but music to the others,
Music as of birds afar off,
Of the whippoorwill afar off,
Of the lonely Wawonaissa
Singing in the darksome forest.

"Then the lodge began to tremble,
Straight began to shake and tremble,
And they felt it rising, rising,
Slowly through the air ascending,
From the darkness of the tree-tops
Forth into the dewy starlight,
Till it passed the topmost branches;
And behold! the wooden dishes
All were changed to shells of scarlet!
And behold! the earthen kettles
All were changed to bowls of silver!
And the roof-poles of the wigwam
Were as glittering rods of silver,
And the roof of bark upon them
As the shining shards of beetles.

"Then Osseo gazed around him,
And he saw the nine fair sisters,

All the sisters and their husbands,
Changed to birds of various plumage.
Some were jays and some were magpies,
Others thrushes, others blackbirds;
And they hopped, and sang, and twittered,
Perked and fluttered all their feathers,
Strutted in their shining plumage,
And their tails like fans unfolded.

  "Only Oweenee, the youngest,
Was not changed, but sat in silence,
Wasted, wrinkled, old, and ugly,
Looking sadly at the others;
Till Osseo, gazing upward,
Gave another cry of anguish,
Such a cry as he had uttered
By the oak-tree in the forest.

  "Then returned her youth and beauty,
And her soiled and tattered garments
Were transformed to robes of ermine,
And her staff became a feather,
Yes, a shining silver feather!

  "And again the wigwam trembled,
Swayed and rushed through airy currents,
Through transparent cloud and vapor,

And amid celestial splendors
On the Evening Star alighted,
As a snow-flake falls on snow-flake,
As a leaf drops on a river,
As the thistle-down on water.

"Forth with cheerful words of welcome
Came the father of Osseo,
He with radiant locks of silver,
He with eyes serene and tender.
And he said: 'My son, Osseo,
Hang the cage of birds you bring there,
Hang the cage with rods of silver,
And the birds with glistening feathers,
At the doorway of my wigwam.'

"At the door he hung the bird-cage,
And they entered in and gladly
Listened to Osseo's father,
Ruler of the Star of Evening,
As he said: 'O my Osseo!
I have had compassion on you,
Given you back your youth and beauty,
Into birds of various plumage
Changed your sisters and their husbands;
Changed them thus because they mocked you,

In the figure of the old man,
In that aspect sad and wrinkled,
Could not see your heart of passion,
Could not see your youth immortal;
Only Oweenee, the faithful,
Saw your naked heart and loved you.

    " ' In the lodge that glimmers yonder
In the little star that twinkles
Through the vapors, on the left hand,
Lives the envious Evil Spirit,
The Wabeno, the magician,
Who transformed you to an old man.
Take heed lest his beams fall on you,
For the rays he darts around him
Are the power of his enchantment,
Are the arrows that he uses.'

    "Many years, in peace and quiet,
On the peaceful Star of Evening
Dwelt Osseo with his father;
Many years, in song and flutter,
At the doorway of the wigwam,
Hung the cage with rods of silver,
And fair Oweenee, the faithful,
Bore a son unto Osseo,

With the beauty of his mother,
With the courage his father.

"And the boy grew up and prospered,
And Osseo, to delight him,
Made him little bows and arrows,
Opened the great cage of silver,
And let loose his aunts and uncles,
All those birds with glossy feathers,
For his little son to shoot at.

"Round and round they wheeled and
    darted,
Filled the Evening Star with music,
With their songs of joy and freedom;
Filled the Evening Star with splendor,
With the fluttering of their plumage;
Till the boy, the little hunter,
Bent his bow and shot an arrow,
Shot a swift and fatal arrow,
And a bird, with shining feathers,
At his feet fell wounded sorely.

"But, O wondrous transformation!
'T was no bird he saw before him,
'T was a beautiful young woman,
With the arrow in her bosom!

"When her blood fell on the planet,
On the sacred Star of Evening,
Broken was the spell of magic,
Powerless was the strange enchantment,
And the youth, the fearless bowman,
Suddenly felt himself descending,
Held by unseen hands, but sinking
Downward through the empty spaces,
Downward through the clouds and vapors,
Till he rested on an island,
On an island, green and grassy,
Yonder in the Big-Sea-Water.

"After him he saw descending
All the birds with shining feathers,
Fluttering, falling, wafted downward,
Like the painted leaves of Autumn;
And the lodge with poles of silver,
With its roof like wings of beetles,
Like the shining shards of beetles,
By the winds of heaven uplifted,
Slowly sank upon the island,
Bringing back the good Osseo,
Bringing Oweenee, the faithful.

"Then the birds, again transfigured,

Reassumed the shape of mortals,
Took their shape, but not their stature;
They remained as Little People,
Like the pigmies, the Puk-Wudjies,
And on pleasant nights of Summer,
When the Evening Star was shining,
Hand in hand they danced together
On the island's craggy headlands,
On the sand-beach low and level.

"Still their glittering lodge is seen there,
On the tranquil Summer evenings,
And upon the shore the fisher
Sometimes hears their happy voices,
Sees them dancing in the starlight!"

When the story was completed,
When the wondrous tale was ended,
Looking round upon his listeners,
Solemnly Iagoo added:
"There are great men, I have known such,
Whom their people understand not,
Whom they even make a jest of,
Scoff and jeer at in derision.
From the story of Osseo
Let them learn the fate of jesters!"

All the wedding guests delighted
Listened to the marvellous story,
Listened laughing and applauding,
And they whispered to each other:
"Does he mean himself, I wonder?
And are we the aunts and uncles?"

Then again sang Chibiabos,
Sang a song of love and longing,
In those accents sweet and tender,
In those tones of pensive sadness,
Sang a maiden's lamentation
For her lover, her Algonquin.

"When I think of my belovéd,
Ah me! think of my belovéd,
When my heart is thinking of him,
O my sweetheart, my Algonquin!

"Ah me! when I parted from him,
Round my neck he hung the wampum,
As a pledge, the snow-white wampum,
O my sweetheart, my Algonquin!

"I will go with you, he whispered,
Ah me! to your native country;
Let me go with you, he whispered,
O my sweetheart, my Algonquin!

"Far away, away, I answered,
Very far away, I answered,
Ah me! is my native country,
O my sweetheart, my Algonquin!

"When I looked back to behold him,
Where we parted, to behold him,
After me he still was gazing,
O my sweetheart, my Algonquin!

"By the tree he still was standing,
By the fallen tree was standing,
That had dropped into the water,
O my sweetheart, my Algonquin!

"When I think of my belovéd,
Ah me! think of my belovéd,
When my heart is thinking of him,
O my sweetheart, my Algonquin!"

Such was Hiawatha's Wedding,
Such the dance of Pau-Puk-Keewis,
Such the story of Iagoo,
Such the songs of Chibiabos;
Thus the wedding banquet ended,
And the wedding guests departed,
Leaving Hiawatha happy
With the night and Minnehaha.

## XIII.

### BLESSING THE CORN–FIELDS.

SING, O Song of Hiawatha,
Of the happy days that followed,
In the land of the Ojibways,
In the pleasant land and peaceful!
Sing the mysteries of Mondamin,
Sing the Blessing of the Corn-fields!
  Buried was the bloody hatchet,
Buried was the dreadful war-club,
Buried were all warlike weapons,
And the war-cry was forgotten.
There was peace among the nations;
Unmolested roved the hunters,
Built the birch canoe for sailing,
Caught the fish in lake and river,
Shot the deer and trapped the beaver;
Unmolested worked the women,

Made their sugar from the maple,
Gathered wild rice in the meadows,
Dressed the skins of deer and beaver.

All around the happy village
Stood the maize-fields, green and shining,
Waved the green plumes of Mondamin,
Waved his soft and sunny tresses,
Filling all the land with plenty.
'T was the women who in Spring-time
Planted the broad fields and fruitful,
Buried in the earth Mondamin;
'T was the women who in Autumn
Stripped the yellow husks of harvest,
Stripped the garments from Mondamin,
Even as Hiawatha taught them.

Once, when all the maize was planted,
Hiawatha, wise and thoughtful,
Spake and said to Minnehaha,
To his wife, the Laughing Water:
"You shall bless to-night the corn-fields,
Draw a magic circle round them,
To protect them from destruction,
Blast of mildew, blight of insect,
Wagemin, the thief of corn-fields,

Paimosaid, who steals the maize-ear!
"In the night, when all is silence,
In the night, when all is darkness,
When the Spirit of Sleep, Nepahwin,
Shuts the doors of all the wigwams,
So that not an ear can hear you,
So that not an eye can see you,
Rise up from your bed in silence,
Lay aside your garments wholly,
Walk around the fields you planted,
Round the borders of the corn-fields,
Covered by your tresses only,
Robed with darkness as a garment.

"Thus the fields shall be more fruitful,
And the passing of your footsteps
Draw a magic circle round them,
So that neither blight nor mildew,
Neither burrowing worm nor insect,
Shall pass o'er the magic circle;
Not the dragon-fly, Kwo-ne-she,
Nor the spider, Subbekashe,
Nor the grasshopper, Pah-puk-keena,
Nor the mighty caterpillar,
Way-muk-kwana, with the bear-skin,

King of all the caterpillars!"
  On the tree-tops near the corn-fields
Sat the hungry crows and ravens,
Kahgahgee, the King of Ravens,
With his band of black marauders.
And they laughed at Hiawatha,
Till the tree-tops shook with laughter,
With their melancholy laughter
At the words of Hiawatha.
"Hear him!" said they; "hear the wise man!
Hear the plots of Hiawatha!"

  When the noiseless night descended
Broad and dark o'er field and forest,
When the mournful Wawonaissa,
Sorrowing sang among the hemlocks,
And the Spirit of Sleep, Nepahwin,
Shut the doors of all the wigwams,
From her bed rose Laughing Water,
Laid aside her garments wholly,
And with darkness clothed and guarded,
Unashamed and unaffrighted,
Walked securely round the corn-fields,
Drew the sacred, magic circle
Of her footprints round the corn-fields.

No one but the Midnight only
Saw her beauty in the darkness,
No one but the Wawonaissa
Heard the panting of her bosom;
Guskewau, the darkness, wrapped her
Closely in his sacred mantle,
So that none might see her beauty,
So that none might boast, "I saw her!"

On the morrow, as the day dawned,
Kahgahgee, the King of Ravens,
Gathered all his black marauders,
Crows and blackbirds, jays and ravens,
Clamorous on the dusky tree-tops,
And descended, fast and fearless
On the fields of Hiawatha,
On the grave of the Mondamin.

"We will drag Mondamin," said they,
"From the grave where he is buried,
Spite of all the magic circles
Laughing Water draws around it,
Spite of all the sacred footprints
Minnehaha stamps upon it!"

But the wary Hiawatha
Ever thoughtful, careful, watchful,

Had o'erheard the scornful laughter
When they mocked him from the tree-tops.
"Kaw!" he said, "my friends the ravens!
Kahgahgee, my King of Ravens!
I will teach you all a lesson
That shall not be soon forgotten!"

He had risen before the daybreak,
He had spread o'er all the corn-fields
Snares to catch the black marauders,
And was lying now in ambush
In the neighboring grove of pine-trees,
Waiting for the crows and blackbirds,
Waiting for the jays and ravens.

Soon they came with caw and clamor,
Rush of wings and cry of voices,
To their work of devastation,
Settling down upon the corn-fields,
Delving deep with beak and talon,
For the body of Mondamin.
And with all their craft and cunning,
All their skill in wiles of warfare,
They perceived no danger near them,
Till their claws became entangled,
Till they found themselves imprisoned

In the snares of Hiawatha.

From his place of ambush came he,
Striding terrible among them,
And so awful was his aspect
That the bravest quailed with terror.
Without mercy he destroyed them
Right and left, by tens and twenties,
And their wretched, lifeless bodies
Hung aloft on poles for scarecrows
Round the consecrated corn-fields,
As a signal of his vengeance,
As a warning to marauders.

Only Kahgahgee, the leader,
Kahgahgee, the King of Ravens,
He alone was spared among them
As a hostage for his people.
With his prisoner-string he bound him,
Led him captive to his wigwam,
Tied him fast with cords of elm-bark
To the ridge-pole of his wigwam.

"Kahgahgee, my raven!" said he,
"You the leader of the robbers,
You the plotter of this mischief,
The contriver of this outrage,

I will keep you, I will hold you,
As a hostage for your people,
As a pledge of good behavior!"

And he left him, grim and sulky,
Sitting in the morning sunshine
On the summit of the wigwam,
Croaking fiercely his displeasure,
Flapping his great sable pinions,
Vainly struggling for his freedom,
Vainly calling on his people!

Summer passed, and Shawondasse
Breathed his sighs o'er all the landscape,
From the South-land sent his ardors,
Wafted kisses warm and tender;
And the maize-field grew and ripened,
Till it stood in all the splendor
Of its garments green and yellow,
Of its tassels and its plumage,
And the maize-ears full and shining
Gleamed from bursting sheaths of verdure.

Then Nokomis, the old woman,
Spake, and said to Minnehaha:
"'T is the Moon when leaves are falling;
All the wild-rice has been gathered,

And the maize is ripe and ready;
Let us gather in the harvest,
Let us wrestle with Mondamin,
Strip him of his plumes and tassels,
Of his garments green and yellow!"

And the merry Laughing Water
Went rejoicing from the wigwam,
With Nokomis, old and wrinkled,
And they called the women round them,
Called the young men and the maidens,
To the harvest of the corn-fields,
To the husking of the maize-ear.

On the border of the forest,
Underneath the fragrant pine-trees,
Sat the old men and the warriors
Smoking in the pleasant shadow.
In uninterrupted silence
Looked they at the gamesome labor
Of the young men and the women;
Listened to their noisy talking,
To their laughter and their singing,
Heard them chattering like the magpies,
Heard them laughing like the blue-jays,
Heard them singing like the robins.

And whene'er some lucky maiden
Found a red ear in the husking,
Found a maize-ear red as blood is,
"Nushka!" cried they all together,
"Nushka! you shall have a sweetheart,
You shall have a handsome husband!"
"Ugh!" the old men all responded
From their seats beneath the pine-trees.

And whene'er a youth or maiden
Found a crooked ear in husking,
Found a maize-ear in the husking
Blighted, mildewed, or misshapen,
Then they laughed and sang together,
Crept and limped about the corn-fields,
Mimicked in their gait and gestures
Some old man, bent almost double,
Singing singly or together:
"Wagemin, the thief of corn-fields!
Paimosaid, the skulking robber!"

Till the corn-fields rang with laughter,
Till from Hiawatha's wigwam
Kahgahgee, the King of Ravens,
Screamed and quivered in his anger,
And from all the neighboring tree-tops

Cawed and croaked the black marauders.
" Ugh ! " the old men all responded,
From their seats beneath the pine-trees !

## XIV.

### PICTURE—WRITING.

In those days said Hiawatha:
"Lo! how all things fade and perish!
From the memory of the old men
Fade away the great traditions,
The achievements of the warriors,
The adventures of the hunters,
All the wisdom of the Medas,
All the craft of the Wabenos,
All the marvellous dreams and visions
Of the Jossakeeds, the Prophets!

"Great men die and are forgotten.
Wise men speak; their words of wisdom
Perish in the ears that hear them,
Do not reach the generations
That, as yet unborn, are waiting
In the great, mysterious darkness

Of the speechless days that shall be!
  "On the grave-posts of our fathers
Are no signs, no figures painted;
Who are in those graves we know not,
Only know they are our fathers.
Of what kith they are and kindred,
From what old, ancestral Totem,
Be it Eagle, Bear, or Beaver,
They descended, this we know not,
Only know they are our fathers.

  "Face to face we speak together,
But we cannot speak when absent,
Cannot send our voices from us
To the friends that dwell afar off;
Cannot send a secret message,
But the bearer learns our secret,
May pervert it, may betray it,
May reveal it unto others."

  Thus said Hiawatha, walking
In the solitary forest,
Pondering, musing in the forest,
On the welfare of his people.

  From his pouch he took his colors,
Took his paints of different colors,

On the smooth bark of a birch-tree
Painted many shapes and figures,
Wonderful and mystic figures,
And each figure had a meaning,
Each some word or thought suggested.

  Gitche Manito the Mighty,
He, the Master of Life, was painted
As an egg, with points projecting
To the four winds of the heavens.
Everywhere is the Great Spirit,
Was the meaning of this symbol.

  Mitche Manito the Mighty,
He the dreadful Spirit of Evil,
As a serpent was depicted,
As Kenabeek, the great serpent.
Very crafty, very cunning,
Is the creeping Spirit of Evil,
Was the meaning of this symbol.

  Life and Death he drew as circles,
Life was white, but Death was darkened;
Sun and moon and stars he painted,
Man and beast, and fish and reptile,
Forests, mountains, lakes, and rivers.

  For the earth he drew a straight line,

For the sky a bow above it;
White the space between for day-time,
Filled with little stars for night-time;
On the left a point for sunrise,
On the right a point for sunset,
On the top a point for noontide,
And for rain and cloudy weather
Waving lines descending from it.

Footprints pointing towards a wigwam
Were a sign of invitation,
Were a sign of guests assembling;
Bloody hands with palms uplifted
Were a symbol of destruction,
Were a hostile sign and symbol.

All these things did Hiawatha
Show unto his wondering people,
And interpreted their meaning,
And he said: "Behold, your grave-posts
Have no mark, no sign, nor symbol.
Go and paint them all with figures;
Each one with its household symbol,
With its own ancestral Totem;
So that those who follow after
May distinguish them and know them."

And they painted on the grave-posts
Of the graves yet unforgotten,
Each his own ancestral Totem,
Each the symbol of his household;
Figures of the Bear and Reindeer,
Of the Turtle, Crane, and Beaver,
Each inverted as a token
That the owner was departed,
That the chief who bore the symbol
Lay beneath in dust and ashes.

And the Jossakeeds, the Prophets,
The Wabenos, the Magicians,
And the Medicine-men, the Medas,
Painted upon bark and deer-skin
Figures for the songs they chanted,
For each song a separate symbol,
Figures mystical and awful,
Figures strange and brightly colored;
And each figure had its meaning,
Each some magic song suggested.

The Great Spirit, the Creator,
Flashing light through all the heaven;
The Great Serpent, the Kenabeek,
With his bloody crest erected,

Creeping, looking into heaven;
In the sky the sun, that listens,
And the moon eclipsed and dying;
Owl and eagle, crane and hen-hawk,
And the cormorant, bird of magic;
Headless men, that walk the heavens,
Bodies lying pierced with arrows,
Bloody hands of death uplifted,
Flags on graves, and great war-captains
Grasping both the earth and heaven!

Such as these the shapes they painted
On the birch-bark and the deer-skin;
Songs of war and songs of hunting,
Songs of medicine and of magic,
All were written in these figures,
For each figure had its meaning,
Each its separate song recorded.

Nor forgotten was the Love-Song,
The most subtle of all medicines,
The most potent spell of magic,
Dangerous more than war or hunting!
Thus the Love-Song was recorded,
Symbol and interpretation.

First a human figure standing,

Painted in the brightest scarlet;
'T is the lover, the musician,
And the meaning is: "My painting
Makes me powerful over others."

Then the figure seated, singing,
Playing on a drum of magic,
And the interpretation: "Listen!
'T is my voice you hear, my singing!"

Then the same red figure seated
In the shelter of a wigwam,
And the meaning of the symbol:
"I will come and sit beside you
In the mystery of my passion!"

Then two figures, man and woman,
Standing hand in hand together,
With their hands so clasped together
That they seem in one united,
And the words thus represented
Are: "I see your heart within you,
And your cheeks are red with blushes!"

Next the maiden on an island,
In the centre of an island;
And the song this shape suggested
Was: "Though you were at a distance,

Were upon some far-off island,
Such the spell I cast upon you,
Such the magic power of passion,
I could straightway draw you to me!"

Then the figure of the maiden
Sleeping, and the lover near her,
Whispering to her in her slumbers,
Saying: "Though you were far from me
In the land of Sleep and Silence,
Still the voice of love would reach you!"

And the last of all the figures
Was a heart within a circle,
Drawn within a magic circle;
And the image had this meaning:
"Naked lies your heart before me,
To your naked heart I whisper!"

Thus it was that Hiawatha,
In his wisdom, taught the people
All the mysteries of painting,
All the art of Picture-Writing,
On the smooth bark of the birch-tree,
On the white skin of the reindeer,
On the grave-posts of the village.

## XV.

### HIAWATHA'S LAMENTATION.

In those days the Evil Spirits,
All the Manitos of mischief,
Fearing Hiawatha's wisdom,
And his love for Chibiabos,
Jealous of their faithful friendship,
And their noble words and actions,
Made at length a league against them,
To molest them and destroy them.

 Hiawatha, wise and wary,
Often said to Chibiabos:
"O my brother! do not leave me,
Lest the Evil Spirits harm you!"
Chibiabos, young and heedless,
Laughing shook his coal-black tresses,
Answered ever sweet and childlike:
"Do not fear for me, O brother!

Harm and evil come not near me!"

Once when Peboan, the Winter,
Roofed with ice the Big-Sea-Water,
When the snow-flakes, whirling downward,
Hissed among the withered oak-leaves,
Changed the pine-trees into wigwams,
Covered all the earth with silence, —
Armed with arrows, shod with snow-shoes,
Heeding not his brother's warning,
Fearing not the Evil Spirits,
Forth to hunt the deer with antlers
All alone went Chibiabos.

Right across the Big-Sea-Water
Sprang with speed the deer before him.
With the wind and snow he followed,
O'er the treacherous ice he followed,
Wild with all the fierce commotion
And the rapture of the hunting.

But beneath, the Evil Spirits
Lay in ambush, waiting for him,
Broke the treacherous ice beneath him,
Dragged him downward to the bottom,
Buried in the sand his body.
Unktahee, the god of water,

He the god of the Dacotahs,
Drowned him in the deep abysses
Of the lake of Gitche Gumee.

From the headlands Hiawatha
Sent forth such a wail of anguish,
Such a fearful lamentation,
That the bison paused to listen,
And the wolves howled from the prairies,
And the thunder in the distance
Woke and answered "Baim-wawa!"

Then his face with black he painted,
With his robe his head he covered,
In his wigwam sat lamenting,
Seven long weeks he sat lamenting,
Uttering still this moan of sorrow:—

"He is dead, the sweet musician!
He the sweetest of all singers!
He has gone from us for ever,
He has moved a little nearer
To the Master of all music,
To the Master of all singing!
O my brother, Chibiabos!"

And the melancholy fir-trees
Waved their dark green fans above him,

Waved their purple cones above him,
Sighing with him to console him,
Mingling with his lamentation
Their complaining, their lamenting.

Came the Spring, and all the forest
Looked in vain for Chibiabos;
Sighed the rivulet, Sebowisha,
Sighed the rushes in the meadow.

From the tree-tops sang the blue-bird,
Sang the blue-bird, the Owaissa:
"Chibiabos! Chibiabos!
He is dead, the sweet musician!"

From the wigwam sang the robin,
Sang the Opechee, the robin:
"Chibiabos! Chibiabos!
He is dead, the sweetest singer!"

And at night through all the forest
Went the whippoorwill complaining,
Wailing went the Wawonaissa:
"Chibiabos! Chibiabos!
He is dead, the sweet musician!
He the sweetest of all singers!"

Then the medicine-men, the Medas,
The magicians, the Wabenos,

And the Jossakeeds, the prophets,
Came to visit Hiawatha;
Built a Sacred Lodge beside him,
To appease him, to console him,
Walked in silent, grave procession,
Bearing each a pouch of healing,
Skin of beaver, lynx, or otter,
Filled with magic roots and simples,
Filled with very potent medicines.

When he heard their steps approaching,
Hiawatha ceased lamenting,
Called no more on Chibiabos;
Naught he questioned, naught he answered,
But his mournful head uncovered,
From his face the mourning colors
Washed he slowly and in silence,
Slowly and in silence followed
Onward to the Sacred Wigwam.

There a magic drink they gave him,
Made of Nahma-wusk, the spearmint,
And Wabeno-wusk, the yarrow,
Roots of power, and herbs of healing;
Beat their drums, and shook their rattles;
Chanted singly and in chorus,

Mystic songs like these, they chanted:
  "I myself, myself! behold me!
'T is the great Gray Eagle talking;
Come, ye white crows, come and hear him!
The loud-speaking thunder helps me;
All the unseen spirits help me;
I can hear their voices calling,
All around the sky I hear them!
I can blow you strong, my brother,
I can heal you, Hiawatha!"

  "Hi-au-ha!" replied the chorus,
"Way-ha-way!" the mystic chorus.

  "Friends of mine are all the serpents!
Hear me shake my skin of hen-hawk!
Mahng, the white loon, I can kill him;
I can shoot your heart and kill it!
I can blow you strong, my brother,
I can heal you, Hiawatha!"

  "Hi-au-ha!" replied the chorus,
"Way-ha-way!" the mystic chorus.

  "I myself, myself! the prophet!
When I speak the wigwam trembles,
Shakes the Sacred Lodge with terror,
Hands unseen begin to shake it!

When I walk, the sky I tread on
Bends and makes a noise beneath me!
I can blow you strong, my brother!
Rise and speak, O Hiawatha!"

"Hi-au-ha!" replied the chorus,
"Way-ha-way!" the mystic chorus.

Then they shook their medicine-pouches
O'er the head of Hiawatha,
Danced their medicine-dance around him;
And upstarting wild and haggard,
Like a man from dreams awakened,
He was healed of all his madness.
As the clouds are swept from heaven,
Straightway from his brain departed
All his moody melancholy;
As the ice is swept from rivers,
Straightway from his heart departed
All his sorrow and affliction.

Then they summoned Chibiabos
From his grave beneath the waters,
From the sands of Gitche Gumee
Summoned Hiawatha's brother.
And so mighty was the magic
Of that cry and invocation,

That he heard it as he lay there
Underneath the Big-Sea-Water;
From the sand he rose and listened,
Heard the music and the singing,
Came, obedient to the summons,
To the doorway of the wigwam,
But to enter they forbade him.

Through a chink a coal they gave him,
Through the door a burning fire-brand;
Ruler in the Land of Spirits,
Ruler o'er the dead, they made him,
Telling him a fire to kindle
For all those that died thereafter,
Camp-fires for their night encampments
On their solitary journey
To the kingdom of Ponemah,
To the land of the Hereafter.

From the village of his childhood,
From the homes of those who knew him,
Passing silent through the forest,
Like a smoke-wreath wafted sideways,
Slowly vanished Chibiabos!
Where he passed, the branches moved not,
Where he trod, the grasses bent not,

And the fallen leaves of last year
Made no sound beneath his footsteps.

    Four whole days he journeyed onward
Down the pathway of the dead men;
On the dead-man's strawberry feasted,
Crossed the melancholy river,
On the swinging log he crossed it,
Came unto the Lake of Silver,
In the Stone Canoe was carried
To the Islands of the Blessed,
To the land of ghosts and shadows.

    On that journey, moving slowly,
Many weary spirits saw he,
Panting under heavy burdens,
Laden with war-clubs, bows and arrows,
Robes of fur, and pots and kettles,
And with food that friends had given
For that solitary journey.

    "Ah! why do the living," said they,
"Lay such heavy burdens on us!
Better were it to go naked,
Better were it to go fasting,
Than to bear such heavy burdens
On our long and weary journey!"

Forth then issued Hiawatha,
Wandered eastward, wandered westward,
Teaching men the use of simples
And the antidotes for poisons,
And the cure of all diseases.
Thus was first made known to mortals
All the mystery of Medamin,
All the sacred art of healing.

## XVI.

### PAU–PUK–KEEWIS.

You shall hear how Pau-Puk-Keewis
He, the handsome Yenadizze,
Whom the people called the Storm Fool,
Vexed the village with disturbance;
You shall hear of all his mischief,
And his flight from Hiawatha,
And his wondrous transmigrations,
And the end of his adventures.

On the shores of Gitche Gumee,
On the dunes of Nagow Wudjoo,
By the shining Big-Sea-Water
Stood the lodge of Pau-Puk-Keewis.
It was he who in his frenzy
Whirled these drifting sands together,
On the dunes of Nagow Wudjoo,
When, among the guests assembled,

He so merrily and madly
Danced at Hiawatha's wedding,
Danced the Beggar's Dance to please them.

Now, in search of new adventures,
From his lodge went Pau-Puk-Keewis,
Came with speed into the village,
Found the young men all assembled
In the lodge of old Iagoo,
Listening to his monstrous stories,
To his wonderful adventures.

He was telling them the story
Of Ojeeg, the Summer-Maker,
How he made a hole in heaven,
How he climbed up into heaven,
And let out the Summer-weather,
The perpetual, pleasant Summer;
How the Otter first essayed it;
How the Beaver, Lynx, and Badger
Tried in turn the great achievement,
From the summit of the mountain
Smote their fists against the heavens,
Smote against the sky their foreheads,
Cracked the sky, but could not break it;
How the Wolverine, uprising,

Made him ready for the encounter,
Bent his knees down, like a squirrel,
Drew his arms back, like a cricket.

"Once he leaped," said old Iagoo,
"Once he leaped, and lo! above him
Bent the sky, as ice in rivers
When the waters rise beneath it;
Twice he leaped, and lo! above him
Cracked the sky, as ice in rivers
When the freshet is at highest!
Thrice he leaped, and lo! above him
Broke the shattered sky asunder,
And he disappeared within it,
And Ojeeg, the Fisher Weasel,
With a bound went in behind him!"

"Hark you!" shouted Pau-Puk-Keewis
As he entered at the doorway;
"I am tired of all this talking,
Tired of old Iagoo's stories,
Tired of Hiawatha's wisdom.
Here is something to amuse you,
Better than this endless talking."

Then from out his pouch of wolf-skin
Forth he drew, with solemn manner,

All the game of Bowl and Counters,
Pugasaing, with thirteen pieces.
White on one side were they painted,
And vermilion on the other;
Two Kenabeeks or great serpents,
Two Ininewug or wedge-men,
One great war-club, Puggawaugun,
And one slender fish, the Keego,
Four round pieces, Ozawabeeks,
And three Sheshebwug or ducklings.
All were made of bone and painted,
All except the Ozawabeeks;
These were brass, on one side burnished,
And were black upon the other.

In a wooden bowl he placed them,
Shook and jostled them together,
Threw them on the ground before him,
Thus exclaiming and explaining:
"Red side up are all the pieces,
And one great Kenabeek standing
On the bright side of a brass piece,
On a burnished Ozawabeek;
Thirteen tens and eight are counted."

Then again he shook the pieces,

Shook and jostled them together,
Threw them on the ground before him,
Still exclaiming and explaining:
"White are both the great Kenabeeks,
White the Ininewug, the wedge-men,
Red are all the other pieces;
Five tens and an eight are counted."

Thus he taught the game of hazard,
Thus displayed it and explained it,
Running through its various chances,
Various changes, various meanings:
Twenty curious eyes stared at him,
Full of eagerness stared at him.

"Many games," said old Iagoo,
"Many games of skill and hazard
Have I seen in different nations,
Have I played in different countries.
He who plays with old Iagoo
Must have very nimble fingers·
Though you think yourself so skilful
I can beat you, Pau-Puk-Keewis,
I can even give you lessons
In your game of Bowl and Counters!"

So they sat and played together,

All the old men and the young men,
Played for dresses, weapons, wampum,
Played till midnight, played till morning,
Played until the Yenadizze,
Till the cunning Pau-Puk-Keewis,
Of their treasures had despoiled them,
Of the best of all their dresses,
Shirts of deer-skin, robes of ermine,
Belts of wampum, crests of feathers,
Warlike weapons, pipes and pouches.
Twenty eyes glared wildly at him,
Like the eyes of wolves glared at him.

Said the lucky Pau-Puk-Keewis:
"In my wigwam I am lonely,
In my wanderings and adventures
I have need of a companion,
Fain would have a Meshinauwa
An attendant and pipe-bearer.
I will venture all these winnings,
All these garments heaped about me,
All this wampum, all these feathers,
On a single throw will venture
All against the young man yonder!"
'T was a youth of sixteen summers,

'T was a nephew of Iagoo;
Face-in-a-Mist, the people called him.

As the fire burns in a pipe-head
Dusky red beneath the ashes,
So beneath his shaggy eyebrows
Glowed the eyes of old Iagoo.
"Ugh!" he answered very fiercely;
"Ugh!" they answered all and each one.

Seized the wooden bowl the old man,
Closely in his bony fingers
Clutched the fatal bowl, Onagon,
Shook it fiercely and with fury,
Made the pieces ring together
As he threw them down before him.

Red were both the great Kenabeeks,
Red the Ininewug, the wedge-men,
Red the Sheshebwug, the ducklings,
Black the four brass Ozawabeeks,
White alone the fish, the Keego;
Only five the pieces counted!

Then the smiling Pau-Puk-Keewis
Shook the bowl and threw the pieces;
Lightly in the air he tossed them,
And they fell about him scattered;

Dark and bright the Ozawabeeks,
Red and white the other pieces,
And upright among the others
One Ininewug was standing,
Even as crafty Pau-Puk-Keewis
Stood alone among the players,
Saying, "Five tens! mine the game is!"

Twenty eyes glared at him fiercely,
Like the eyes of wolves glared at him,
As he turned and left the wigwam,
Followed by his Meshinauwa,
By the nephew of Iagoo,
By the tall and graceful stripling,
Bearing in his arms the winnings,
Shirts of deer-skin, robes of ermine,
Belts of wampum, pipes and weapons.

"Carry them," said Pau-Puk-Keewis,
Pointing with his fan of feathers,
"To my wigwam far to eastward,
On the dunes of Nagow Wudjoo!"

Hot and red with smoke and gambling
Were the eyes of Pau-Puk-Keewis
As he came forth to the freshness
Of the pleasant Summer morning.

All the birds were singing gayly,
All the streamlets flowing swiftly,
And the heart of Pau-Puk-Keewis
Sang with pleasure as the birds sing,
Beat with triumph like the streamlets,
As he wandered through the village,
In the early gray of morning,
With his fan of turkey-feathers,
With his plumes and tufts of swan's down,
Till he reached the farthest wigwam,
Reached the lodge of Hiawatha.

Silent was it and deserted;
No one met him at the doorway,
No one came to bid him welcome;
But the birds were singing round it,
In and out and round the doorway,
Hopping, singing, fluttering, feeding,
And aloft upon the ridge-pole
Kahgahgee, the King of Ravens,
Sat with fiery eyes, and, screaming,
Flapped his wings at Pau-Puk-Keewis.

"All are gone! the lodge is empty!"
Thus it was spake Pau-Puk-Keewis,
In his heart resolving mischief;—

"Gone is wary Hiawatha,
Gone the silly Laughing Water,
Gone Nokomis, the old woman,
And the lodge is left unguarded!"

By the neck he seized the raven,
Whirled it round him like a rattle,
Like a medicine-pouch he shook it,
Strangled Kahgahgee, the raven,
From the ridge-pole of the wigwam
Left its lifeless body hanging,
As an insult to its master,
As a taunt to Hiawatha.

With a stealthy step he entered,
Round the lodge in wild disorder
Threw the household things about him,
Piled together in confusion
Bowls of wood and earthen kettles,
Robes of buffalo and beaver,
Skins of otter, lynx, and ermine,
As an insult to Nokomis,
As a taunt to Minnehaha.

Then departed Pau-Puk-Keewis,
Whistling, singing through the forest,
Whistling gayly to the squirrels,

Who from hollow boughs above him
Dropped their acorn-shells upon him,
Singing gayly to the wood-birds,
Who from out the leafy darkness
Answered with a song as merry.

Then he climbed the rocky headlands,
Looking o'er the Gitche Gumee,
Perched himself upon their summit,
Waiting full of mirth and mischief
The return of Hiawatha.

Stretched upon his back he lay there;
Far below him plashed the waters,
Plashed and washed the dreamy waters;
Far above him swam the heavens,
Swam the dizzy, dreamy heavens;
Round him hovered, fluttered, rustled,
Hiawatha's mountain chickens,
Flock-wise swept and wheeled about him,
Almost brushed him with their pinions.

And he killed them as he lay there,
Slaughtered them by tens and twenties,
Threw their bodies down the headland,
Threw them on the beach below him,
Till at length Kayoshk, the sea-gull,

Perched upon a crag above them,
Shouted: "It is Pau-Puk-Keewis!
He is slaying us by hundreds!
Send a message to our brother,
Tidings send to Hiawatha!"

## XVII.

### THE HUNTING OF PAU—PUK—KEEWIS.

FULL of wrath was Hiawatha
When he came into the village,
Found the people in confusion,
Heard of all the misdemeanors,
All the malice and the mischief,
Of the cunning Pau-Puk-Keewis.

Hard his breath came through his nostrils,
Through his teeth he buzzed and muttered
Words of anger and resentment,
Hot and humming, like a hornet.
"I will slay this Pau-Puk-Keewis,
Slay this mischief-maker!" said he.
"Not so long and wide the world is,
Not so rude and rough the way is,
That my wrath shall not attain him,
That my vengeance shall not reach him!"

Then in swift pursuit departed
Hiawatha and the hunters
On the trail of Pau-Puk-Keewis,
Through the forest, where he passed it,
To the headlands where he rested;
But they found not Pau-Puk-Keewis,
Only in the trampled grasses,
In the whortleberry-bushes,
Found the couch where he had rested,
Found the impress of his body.

From the lowlands far beneath them,
From the Muskoday, the meadow,
Pau-Puk-Keewis, turning backward,
Made a gesture of defiance,
Made a gesture of derision;
And aloud cried Hiawatha,
From the summit of the mountain:
"Not so long and wide the world is,
Not so rude and rough the way is,
But my wrath shall overtake you,
And my vengeance shall attain you!"

Over rock and over river,
Thorough bush, and brake, and forest,
Ran the cunning Pau-Puk-Keewis;

Like an antelope he bounded,
Till he came unto a streamlet
In the middle of the forest,
To a streamlet still and tranquil,
That had overflowed its margin,
To a dam made by the beavers,
To a pond of quiet water,
Where knee-deep the trees were standing,
Where the water-lilies floated,
Where the rushes waved and whispered.

On the dam stood Pau-Puk-Keewis,
On the dam of trunks and branches,
Through whose chinks the water spouted,
O'er whose summit flowed the streamlet.
From the bottom rose a beaver,
Looked with two great eyes of wonder,
Eyes that seemed to ask a question,
At the stranger, Pau-Puk-Keewis.

On the dam stood Pau-Puk-Keewis,
O'er his ankles flowed the streamlet,
Flowed the bright and silvery water,
And he spake unto the beaver,
With a smile he spake in this wise:

"O my friend Ahmeek, the beaver,

Cool and pleasant is the water;
Let me dive into the water,
Let me rest there in your lodges;
Change me, too, into a beaver!"

Cautiously replied the beaver,
With reserve he thus made answer:
"Let me first consult the others,
Let me ask the other beavers."
Down he sank into the water,
Heavily sank he, as a stone sinks,
Down among the leaves and branches,
Brown and matted at the bottom.

On the dam stood Pau-Puk-Keewis,
O'er his ankles flowed the streamlet,
Spouted through the chinks below him,
Dashed upon the stones beneath him,
Spread serene and calm before him,
And the sunshine and the shadows
Fell in flecks and gleams upon him,
Fell in little shining patches,
Through the waving, rustling branches.

From the bottom rose the beavers,
Silently above the surface
Rose one head and then another,

Till the pond seemed full of beavers,
Full of black and shining faces.

  To the beavers Pau-Puk-Keewis
Spake entreating, said in this wise:
"Very pleasant is your dwelling,
O my friends! and safe from danger;
Can you not with all your cunning,
All your wisdom and contrivance,
Change me, too, into a beaver?"

  "Yes!" replied Ahmeek, the beaver,
He the King of all the beavers,
"Let yourself slide down among us,
Down into the tranquil water."

  Down into the pond among them
Silently sank Pau-Puk-Keewis;
Black became his shirt of deer-skin,
Black his moccasins and leggings,
In a broad black tail behind him
Spread his fox-tails and his fringes;
He was changed into a beaver.

  "Make me large," said Pau-Puk-Keewis,
"Make me large and make me larger,
Larger than the other beavers."
"Yes," the beaver chief responded,

"When our lodge below you enter,
In our wigwam we will make you
Ten times larger than the others."

Thus into the clear, brown water
Silently sank Pau-Puk-Keewis;
Found the bottom covered over
With the trunks of trees and branches,
Hoards of food against the winter,
Piles and heaps against the famine,
Found the lodge with arching doorway,
Leading into spacious chambers.

Here they made him large and larger
Made him largest of the beavers,
Ten times larger than the others.
"You shall be our ruler," said they;
"Chief and king of all the beavers."

But not long had Pau-Puk-Keewis
Sat in state among the beavers,
When there came a voice of warning
From the watchman at his station
In the water-flags and lilies,
Saying: "Here is Hiawatha!
Hiawatha with his hunters!"

Then they heard a cry above them,

Heard a shouting and a tramping,
Heard a crashing and a rushing,
And the water round and o'er them
Sank and sucked away in eddies,
And they knew their dam was broken.

On the lodge's roof the hunters
Leaped, and broke it all asunder;
Streamed the sunshine through the crevice,
Sprang the beavers through the doorway,
Hid themselves in deeper water,
In the channel of the streamlet;
But the mighty Pau-Puk-Keewis
Could not pass beneath the doorway;
He was puffed with pride and feeding,
He was swollen like a bladder.

Through the roof looked Hiawatha,
Cried aloud: "O Pau-Puk-Keewis!
Vain are all your craft and cunning,
Vain your manifold disguises!
Well I know you, Pau-Puk-Keewis!"

With their clubs they beat and bruised him,
Beat to death poor Pau-Puk-Keewis,
Pounded him as maize is pounded,
Till his skull was crushed to pieces.

Six tall hunters, lithe and limber,
Bore him home on poles and branches,
Bore the body of the beaver;
But the ghost, the Jeebi in him,
Thought and felt as Pau-Puk-Keewis,
Still lived on as Pau-Puk-Keewis.

And it fluttered, strove, and struggled,
Waving hither, waving thither,
As the curtains of a wigwam
Struggle with their thongs of deer-skin,
When the wintry wind is blowing;
Till it drew itself together,
Till it rose up from the body,
Till it took the form and features
Of the cunning Pau-Puk-Keewis,
Vanishing into the forest.

But the wary Hiawatha
Saw the figure ere it vanished,
Saw the form of Pau-Puk-Keewis
Glide into the soft blue shadow
Of the pine-trees of the forest;
Toward the squares of white beyond it,
Toward an opening in the forest,
Like a wind it rushed and panted,

Bending all the boughs before it,
And behind it, as the rain comes,
Came the steps of Hiawatha.

To a lake with many islands
Came the breathless Pau-Puk-Keewis,
Where among the water-lilies
Pishnekuh, the brant, were sailing;
Through the tufts of rushes floating,
Steering through the reedy islands.
Now their broad black beaks they lifted,
Now they plunged beneath the water,
Now they darkened in the shadow,
Now they brightened in the sunshine.

"Pishnekuh!" cried Pau-Puk-Keewis,
"Pishnekuh! my brothers!" said he,
"Change me to a brant with plumage,
With a shining neck and feathers,
Make me large, and make me larger,
Ten times larger than the others."

Straightway to a brant they changed him,
With two huge and dusky pinions,
With a bosom smooth and rounded,
With a bill like two great paddles,
Made him larger than the others,

Ten times larger than the largest,
Just as, shouting from the forest,
On the shore stood Hiawatha.

Up they rose with cry and clamor,
With a whirr and beat of pinions,
Rose up from the reedy islands,
From the water-flags and lilies.
And they said to Pau-Puk-Keewis:
"In your flying, look not downward,
Take good heed, and look not downward,
Lest some strange mischance should happen,
Lest some great mishap befall you!"

Fast and far they fled to northward,
Fast and far through mist and sunshine
Fed among the moors and fen-lands,
Slept among the reeds and rushes.

On the morrow as they journeyed,
Buoyed and lifted by the South-wind,
Wafted onward by the South-wind,
Blowing fresh and strong behind them,
Rose a sound of human voices,
Rose a clamor from beneath them,
From the lodges of a village,
From the people miles beneath them.

For the people of the village
Saw the flock of brant with wonder,
Saw the wings of Pau-Puk-Keewis
Flapping far up in the ether,
Broader than two doorway curtains.

Pau-Puk-Keewis heard the shouting,
Knew the voice of Hiawatha,
Knew the outcry of Iagoo,
And, forgetful of the warning,
Drew his neck in, and looked downward,
And the wind that blew behind him
Caught his mighty fan of feathers,
Sent him wheeling, whirling downward!

All in vain did Pau-Puk-Keewis
Struggle to regain his balance!
Whirling round and round and downward,
He beheld in turn the village
And in turn the flock above him,
Saw the village coming nearer,
And the flock receding farther,
Heard the voices growing louder,
Heard the shouting and the laughter;
Saw no more the flock above him,
Only saw the earth beneath him;

Dead out of the empty heaven,
Dead among the shouting people,
With a heavy sound and sullen,
Fell the brant with broken pinions.

But his soul, his ghost, his shadow,
Still survived as Pau-Puk-Keewis,
Took again the form and features
Of the handsome Yenadizze,
And again went rushing onward,
Followed fast by Hiawatha,
Crying: "Not so wide the world is,
Not so long and rough the way is,
But my wrath shall overtake you,
But my vengeance shall attain you!"

And so near he came, so near him,
That his hand was stretched to seize him,
His right hand to seize and hold him,
When the cunning Pau-Puk-Keewis
Whirled and spun about in circles,
Fanned the air into a whirlwind,
Danced the dust and leaves about him,
And amid the whirling eddies
Sprang into a hollow oak-tree,
Changed himself into a serpent,

Gliding out through root and rubbish.

With his right hand Hiawatha
Smote amain the hollow oak-tree,
Rent it into shreds and splinters,
Left it lying there in fragments.
But in vain; for Pau-Puk-Keewis,
Once again in human figure,
Full in sight ran on before him,
Sped away in gust and whirlwind,
On the shores of Gitche Gumee,
Westward by the Big-Sea-Water,
Came unto the rocky headlands,
To the Pictured Rocks of sandstone,
Looking over lake and landscape.

And the Old Man of the Mountain,
He the Manito of Mountains,
Opened wide his rocky doorways,
Opened wide his deep abysses,
Giving Pau-Puk-Keewis shelter
In his caverns dark and dreary,
Bidding Pau-Puk-Keewis welcome
To his gloomy lodge of sandstone.

There without stood Hiawatha,
Found the doorways closed against him,

With his mittens, Minjekahwun,
Smote great caverns in the sandstone,
Cried aloud in tones of thunder:
"Open! I am Hiawatha!"
But the Old Man of the Mountain
Opened not, and made no answer
From the silent crags of sandstone,
From the gloomy rock abysses.

Then he raised his hands to heaven,
Called imploring on the tempest,
Called Waywassimo, the lightning,
And the thunder, Annemeekee;
And they came with night and darkness,
Sweeping down the Big-Sea-Water
From the distant Thunder Mountains;
And the trembling Pau-Puk-Keewis
Heard the footsteps of the thunder,
Saw the red eyes of the lightning,
Was afraid, and crouched and trembled.

Then Waywassimo, the lightning,
Smote the doorways of the caverns,
With his war-club smote the doorways,
Smote the jutting crags of sandstone,
And the thunder, Annemeekee,

Shouted down into the caverns,
Saying: "Where is Pau-Puk-Keewis!"
And the crags fell, and beneath them
Dead among the rocky ruins
Lay the cunning Pau-Puk-Keewis,
Lay the handsome Yenadizze,
Slain in his own human figure.

Ended were his wild adventures,
Ended were his tricks and gambols,
Ended all his craft and cunning,
Ended all his mischief-making,
All his gambling and his dancing,
All his wooing of the maidens.

Then the noble Hiawatha
Took his soul, his ghost, his shadow,
Spake and said: "O Pau-Puk-Keewis!
Never more in human figure
Shall you search for new adventures;
Never more with jest and laughter
Dance the dust and leaves in whirlwinds;
But above there in the heavens
You shall soar and sail in circles;
I will change you to an eagle,
To Keneu, the great War-Eagle,

Chief of all the fowls with feathers,
Chief of Hiawatha's chickens."

And the name of Pau-Puk-Keewis
Lingers still among the people,
Lingers still among the singers,
And among the story-tellers;
And in Winter, when the snow-flakes
Whirl in eddies round the lodges,
When the wind in gusty tumult
O'er the smoke-flue pipes and whistles,
"There," they cry, "comes Pau-Puk-Keewis;
He is dancing through the village,
He is gathering in his harvest!"

## XVIII.

### THE DEATH OF KWASIND.

FAR and wide among the nations
Spread the name and fame of Kwasind;
No man dared to strive with Kwasind,
No man could compete with Kwasind.
But the mischievous Puk-Wudjies,
They the envious Little People,
They the fairies and the pigmies,
Plotted and conspired against him.

"If this hateful Kwasind," said they,
"If this great, outrageous fellow
Goes on thus a little longer,
Tearing everything he touches,
Rending everything to pieces,
Filling all the world with wonder,
What becomes of the Puk-Wudjies?
Who will care for the Puk-Wudjies?"

He will tread us down like mushrooms,
Drive us all into the water,
Give our bodies to be eaten
By the wicked Nee-ba-naw-baigs,
By the Spirits of the water!"

So the angry Little People
All conspired against the Strong Man,
All conspired to murder Kwasind,
Yes, to rid the world of Kwasind,
The audacious, overbearing,
Heartless, haughty, dangerous Kwasind!

Now this wondrous strength of Kwasind
In his crown alone was seated;
In his crown too was his weakness;
There alone could he be wounded,
Nowhere else could weapon pierce him,
Nowhere else could weapon harm him.

Even there the only weapon
That could wound him, that could slay him,
Was the seed-cone of the pine-tree,
Was the blue cone of the fir-tree.
This was Kwasind's fatal secret,
Known to no man among mortals;
But the cunning Little People,

The Puk-Wudjies, knew the secret,
Knew the only way to kill him.

So they gathered cones together,
Gathered seed-cones of the pine-tree,
Gathered blue cones of the fir-tree,
In the woods by Taquamenaw,
Brought them to the river's margin,
Heaped them in great piles together,
Where the red rocks from the margin
Jutting overhang the river.
There they lay in wait for Kwasind,
The malicious Little People.

'T was an afternoon in Summer;
Very hot and still the air was,
Very smooth the gliding river,
Motionless the sleeping shadows:
Insects glistened in the sunshine,
Insects skated on the water,
Filled the drowsy air with buzzing,
With a far-resounding war-cry.

Down the river came the Strong Man,
In his birch canoe came Kwasind,
Floating slowly down the current
Of the sluggish Taquamenaw,

Very languid with the weather,
Very sleepy with the silence.

  From the overhanging branches,
From the tassels of the birch-trees,
Soft the Spirit of Sleep descended;
By his airy hosts surrounded,
His invisible attendants,
Came the Spirit of Sleep, Nepahwin;
Like the burnished Dush-kwo-ne-she,
Like a dragon-fly, he hovered
O'er the drowsy head of Kwasind.

  To his ear there came a murmur
As of waves upon a sea-shore,
As of far-off tumbling waters,
As of winds among the pine-trees;
And he felt upon his forehead
Blows of little airy war-clubs,
Wielded by the slumbrous legions
Of the Spirit of Sleep, Nepahwin,
As of some one breathing on him.

  At the first blow of their war-clubs,
Fell a drowsiness on Kwasind;
At the second blow they smote him,
Motionless his paddle rested;

At the third, before his vision
Reeled the landscape into darkness,
Very sound asleep was Kwasind.

So he floated down the river,
Like a blind man seated upright,
Floated down the Taquamenaw,
Underneath the trembling birch-trees,
Underneath the wooded headlands,
Underneath the war encampment
Of the pigmies, the Puk-Wudjies.

There they stood, all armed and waiting,
Hurled the pine-cones down upon him,
Struck him on his brawny shoulders,
On his crown defenceless struck him.
"Death to Kwasind!" was the sudden
War-cry of the Little People.

And he sideways swayed and tumbled,
Sideways fell into the river,
Plunged beneath the sluggish water
Headlong, as an otter plunges;
And the birch-canoe, abandoned,
Drifted empty down the river,
Bottom upward swerved and drifted:
Nothing more was seen of Kwasind.

But the memory of the Strong Man
Lingered long among the people,
And whenever through the forest
Raged and roared the wintry tempest,
And the branches, tossed and troubled,
Creaked and groaned and split asunder,
"Kwasind!" cried they; "that is Kwasind!
He is gathering in his fire-wood!"

## XIX.

### THE GHOSTS.

NEVER stoops the soaring vulture
On his quarry in the desert,
On the sick or wounded bison,
But another vulture, watching
From his high aerial look-out,
Sees the downward plunge, and follows;
And a third pursues the second,
Coming from the invisible ether,
First a speck, and then a vulture,
Till the air is dark with pinions.

So disasters come not singly;
But as if they watched and waited,
Scanning one another's motions,
When the first descends, the others
Follow, follow, gathering flock-wise
Round their victim, sick and wounded,

First a shadow, then a sorrow,
Till the air is dark with anguish.

Now, o'er all the dreary Northland,
Mighty Peboan, the Winter,
Breathing on the lakes and rivers,
Into stone had changed their waters.
From his hair he shook the snow-flakes,
Till the plains were strewn with whiteness,
One uninterrupted level,
As if, stooping, the Creator
With his hand had smoothed them over.

Through the forest, wide and wailing,
Roamed the hunter on his snow-shoes;
In the village worked the women,
Pounded maize, or dressed the deer-skin;
And the young men played together
On the ice the noisy ball-play,
On the plain the dance of snow-shoes.

One dark evening, after sundown,
In her wigwam Laughing Water
Sat with old Nokomis, waiting
For the steps of Hiawatha
Homeward from the hunt returning.

On their faces gleamed the fire-light,

Painting them with streaks of crimson,
In the eyes of old Nokomis
Glimmered like the watery moonlight,
In the eyes of Laughing Water
Glistened like the sun in water;
And behind them crouched their shadows
In the corners of the wigwam,
And the smoke in wreaths above them
Climbed and crowded through the smoke-flue.

Then the curtain of the doorway
From without was slowly lifted;
Brighter glowed the fire a moment,
And a moment swerved the smoke-wreath,
As two women entered softly,
Passed the doorway uninvited,
Without word of salutation,
Without sign of recognition,
Sat down in the farthest corner,
Crouching low among the shadows.

From their aspect and their garments,
Strangers seemed they in the village;
Very pale and haggard were they,
As they sat there sad and silent,
Trembling, cowering with the shadows.

Was it the wind above the smoke-flue,
Muttering down into the wigwam?
Was it the owl, the Koko-koho,
Hooting from the dismal forest?
Sure a voice said in the silence:
"These are corpses clad in garments,
These are ghosts that come to haunt you,
From the kingdom of Ponemah,
From the land of the Hereafter!"

Homeward now came Hiawatha
From his hunting in the forest,
With the snow upon his tresses,
And the red deer on his shoulders.
At the feet of Laughing Water
Down he threw his lifeless burden;
Nobler, handsomer she thought him,
Than when first he came to woo her,
First threw down the deer before her,
As a token of his wishes,
As a promise of the future.

Then he turned and saw the strangers,
Cowering, crouching with the shadows;
Said within himself: "Who are they?
What strange guests has Minnehaha?"

But he questioned not the strangers,
Only spake to bid them welcome
To his lodge, his food, his fireside.

When the evening meal was ready,
And the deer had been divided,
Both the pallid guests, the strangers,
Springing from among the shadows,
Seized upon the choicest portions,
Seized the white fat of the roebuck,
Set apart for Laughing Water,
For the wife of Hiawatha;
Without asking, without thanking,
Eagerly devoured the morsels,
Flitted back among the shadows
In the corner of the wigwam.

Not a word spake Hiawatha,
Not a motion made Nokomis,
Not a gesture Laughing Water;
Not a change came o'er their features;
Only Minnehaha softly
Whispered, saying: "They are famished;
Let them do what best delights them;
Let them eat, for they are famished."

Many a daylight dawned and darkened,

Many a night shook off the daylight
As the pine shakes off the snow-flakes
From the midnight of its branches;
Day by day the guests unmoving
Sat there silent in the wigwam;
But by night, in storm or starlight,
Forth they went into the forest,
Bringing fire-wood to the wigwam,
Bringing pine-cones for the burning,
Always sad and always silent.

And whenever Hiawatha
Came from fishing or from hunting,
When the evening meal was ready,
And the food had been divided,
Gliding from their darksome corner,
Came the pallid guests, the strangers,
Seized upon the choicest portions
Set aside for Laughing Water,
And without rebuke or question
Flitted back among the shadows.

Never once had Hiawatha
By a word or look reproved them;
Never once had old Nokomis
Made a gesture of impatience;

Never once had Laughing Water
Shown resentment at the outrage.
All had they endured in silence,
That the rights of guest and stranger,
That the virtue of free-giving,
By a look might not be lessened,
By a word might not be broken.

Once at midnight Hiawatha,
Ever wakeful, ever watchful,
In the wigwam, dimly lighted
By the brands that still were burning,
By the glimmering, flickering fire-light,
Heard a sighing, oft repeated,
Heard a sobbing, as of sorrow.

From his couch rose Hiawatha,
From his shaggy hides of bison,
Pushed aside the deer-skin curtain,
Saw the pallid guests, the shadows,
Sitting upright on their couches,
Weeping in the silent midnight.

And he said: "O guests! why is it
That your hearts are so afflicted,
That you sob so in the midnight?
Has perchance the old Nokomis,

Has my wife, my Minnehaha,
Wronged or grieved you by unkindness,
Failed in hospitable duties?"

Then the shadows ceased from weeping,
Ceased from sobbing and lamenting,
And they said, with gentle voices:
"We are ghosts of the departed,
Souls of those who once were with you.
From the realms of Chibiabos
Hither have we come to try you,
Hither have we come to warn you.

"Cries of grief and lamentation
Reach us in the Blessed Islands;
Cries of anguish from the living,
Calling back their friends departed,
Sadden us with useless sorrow.
Therefore have we come to try you;
No one knows us, no one heeds us.
We are but a burden to you,
And we see that the departed
Have no place among the living.

"Think of this, O Hiawatha!
Speak of it to all the people,
That henceforward and for ever

They no more with lamentations
Sadden the souls of the departed
In the Islands of the Blessed.

"Do not lay such heavy burdens
In the graves of those you bury,
Not such weight of furs and wampum,
Not such weight of pots and kettles,
For the spirits faint beneath them.
Only give them food to carry,
Only give them fire to light them.

"Four days is the spirit's journey
To the land of ghosts and shadows,
Four its lonely night encampments;
Four times must their fires be lighted.
Therefore, when the dead are buried,
Let a fire, as night approaches,
Four times on the grave be kindled,
That the soul upon its journey
May not lack the cheerful fire-light,
May not grope about in darkness.

"Farewell, noble Hiawatha!
We have put you to the trial,
To the proof have put your patience,
By the insult of our presence,

By the outrage of our actions,
We have found you great and noble.
Fail not in the greater trial,
Faint not in the harder struggle."

    When they ceased, a sudden darkness
Fell and filled the silent wigwam.
Hiawatha heard a rustle
As of garments trailing by him,
Heard the curtain of the doorway
Lifted by a hand he saw not,
Felt the cold breath of the night air,
For a moment saw the starlight;
But he saw the ghosts no longer,
Saw no more the wandering spirits
From the kingdom of Ponemah,
From the land of the Hereafter.

## XX.

### THE FAMINE.

O THE long and dreary Winter!
O the cold and cruel Winter!
Ever thicker, thicker, thicker
Froze the ice on lake and river,
Ever deeper, deeper, deeper
Fell the snow o'er all the landscape,
Fell the covering snow, and drifted
Through the forest, round the village.

Hardly from his buried wigwam
Could the hunter force a passage;
With his mittens and his snow-shoes
Vainly walked he through the forest,
Sought for bird or beast and found none,
Saw no track of deer or rabbit,
In the snow beheld no footprints,
In the ghastly, gleaming forest

Fell, and could not rise from weakness,
Perished there from cold and hunger.
  O the famine and the fever!
O the wasting of the famine!
O the blasting of the fever!
O the wailing of the children!
O the anguish of the women!
  All the earth was sick and famished;
Hungry was the air around them,
Hungry was the sky above them,
And the hungry stars in heaven
Like the eyes of wolves glared at them!
  Into Hiawatha's wigwam
Came two other guests, as silent
As the ghosts were, and as gloomy,
Waited not to be invited,
Did not parley at the doorway,
Sat there without word of welcome
In the seat of Laughing Water;
Looked with haggard eyes and hollow
At the face of Laughing Water.
  And the foremost said: "Behold me!
I am Famine, Bukadawin!"
And the other said: "Behold me!

I am Fever, Ahkosewin!"
And the lovely Minnehaha
Shuddered as they looked upon her,
Shuddered at the words they uttered,
Lay down on her bed in silence,
Hid her face, but made no answer;
Lay there trembling, freezing, burning
At the looks they cast upon her,
At the fearful words they uttered.

Forth into the empty forest
Rushed the maddened Hiawatha;
In his heart was deadly sorrow,
In his face a stony firmness;
On his brow the sweat of anguish
Started, but it froze and fell not.

Wrapped in furs and armed for hunting,
With his mighty bow of ash-tree,
With his quiver full of arrows,
With his mittens, Minjekahwun,
Into the vast and vacant forest
On his snow-shoes strode he forward.

"Gitche Manito, the Mighty!"
Cried he with his face uplifted
In that bitter hour of anguish,

"Give your children food, O father!
Give us food, or we must perish!
Give me food for Minnehaha,
For my dying Minnehaha!"

Through the far-resounding forest,
Through the forest vast and vacant,
Rang that cry of desolation,
But there came no other answer
Than the echo of his crying,
Than the echo of the woodlands,
"Minnehaha! Minnehaha!"

All day long roved Hiawatha
In that melancholy forest,
Through the shadow of whose thickets,
In the pleasant days of Summer,
Of that ne'er forgotten Summer,
He had brought his young wife homeward
From the land of the Dacotahs;
When the birds sang in the thickets,
And the streamlets laughed and glistened,
And the air was full of fragrance,
And the lovely Laughing Water
Said with voice that did not tremble:
"I will follow you, my husband!"

In the wigwam with Nokomis,
With those gloomy guests, that watched her,
With the Famine and the Fever,
She was lying, the Beloved,
She the dying Minnehaha.

"Hark!" she said; "I hear a rushing,
Hear a roaring and a rushing,
Hear the Falls of Minnehaha
Calling to me from a distance!"
"No, my child!" said old Nokomis,
"'T is the night-wind in the pine-trees!"

"Look!" she said; "I see my father
Standing lonely at his doorway,
Beckoning to me from his wigwam
In the land of the Dacotahs!"
"No, my child!" said old Nokomis,
"'T is the smoke that waves and beckons!"

"Ah!" she said, "the eyes of Pauguk
Glare upon me in the darkness,
I can feel his icy fingers
Clasping mine amid the darkness!
Hiawatha! Hiawatha!"

And the desolate Hiawatha,
Far away amid the forest,

Miles away among the mountains,
Heard that sudden cry of anguish,
Heard the voice of Minnehaha
Calling to him in the darkness:
"Hiawatha! Hiawatha!"

Over snow-fields waste and pathless,
Under snow-encumbered branches,
Homeward hurried Hiawatha,
Empty-handed, heavy-hearted,
Heard Nokomis moaning, wailing:
"Wahonowin! Wahonowin!
Would that I had perished for you,
Would that I were dead as you are!
Wahonowin! Wahonowin!"

And he rushed into the wigwam,
Saw the old Nokomis slowly
Rocking to and fro and moaning,
Saw his lovely Minnehaha
Lying dead and cold before him,
And his bursting heart within him
Uttered such a cry of anguish,
That the forest moaned and shuddered,
That the very stars in heaven
Shook and trembled with his anguish.

Then he sat down, still and speechless,
On the bed of Minnehaha,
At the feet of Laughing Water,
At those willing feet, that never
More would lightly run to meet him,
Never more would lightly follow.

With both hands his face he covered,
Seven long days and nights he sat there,
As if in a swoon he sat there,
Speechless, motionless, unconscious
Of the daylight or the darkness.

Then they buried Minnehaha;
In the snow a grave they made her,
In the forest deep and darksome,
Underneath the moaning hemlocks;
Clothed her in her richest garments,
Wrapped her in her robes of ermine,
Covered her with snow, like ermine;
Thus they buried Minnehaha.

And at night a fire was lighted,
On her grave four times was kindled,
For her soul upon its journey
To the Islands of the Blessed.
From his doorway Hiawatha

Saw it burning in the forest,
Lighting up the gloomy hemlocks;
From his sleepless bed uprising,
From the bed of Minnehaha,
Stood and watched it at the doorway,
That it might not be extinguished,
Might not leave her in the darkness.

"Farewell!" said he, "Minnehaha!
Farewell, O my Laughing Water!
All my heart is buried with you,
All my thoughts go onward with you!
Come not back again to labor,
Come not back again to suffer,
Where the Famine and the Fever
Wear the heart and waste the body.
Soon my task will be completed,
Soon your footsteps I shall follow
To the Islands of the Blessed,
To the Kingdom of Ponemah,
To the Land of the Hereafter!"

## XXI.

### THE WHITE MAN'S FOOT.

In his lodge beside a river,
Close beside a frozen river,
Sat an old man, sad and lonely.
White his hair was as a snow-drift;
Dull and low his fire was burning,
And the old man shook and trembled,
Folded in his Waubewyon,
In his tattered white-skin-wrapper,
Hearing nothing but the tempest
As it roared along the forest,
Seeing nothing but the snow-storm,
As it whirled and hissed and drifted.

All the coals were white with ashes,
And the fire was slowly dying,
As a young man, walking lightly,
At the open doorway entered.

Red with blood of youth his cheeks were,
Soft his eyes, as stars in Spring-time,
Bound his forehead was with grasses,
Bound and plumed with scented grasses;
On his lips a smile of beauty,
Filling all the lodge with sunshine,
In his hand a bunch of blossoms
Filling all the lodge with sweetness.

"Ah, my son!" exclaimed the old man,
"Happy are my eyes to see you.
Sit here on the mat beside me,
Sit here by the dying embers,
Let us pass the night together.
Tell me of your strange adventures,
Of the lands where you have travelled;
I will tell you of my prowess,
Of my many deeds of wonder."

From his pouch he drew his peace-pipe,
Very old and strangely fashioned;
Made of red stone was the pipe-head,
And the stem a reed with feathers;
Filled the pipe with bark of willow,
Placed a burning coal upon it,
Gave it to his guest, the stranger,

And began to speak in this wise:
"When I blow my breath about me,
When I breathe upon the landscape,
Motionless are all the rivers,
Hard as stone becomes the water!"

And the young man answered, smiling:
"When I blow my breath about me,
When I breathe upon the landscape,
Flowers spring up o'er all the meadows,
Singing, onward rush the rivers!"

"When I shake my hoary tresses,"
Said the old man darkly frowning,
"All the land with snow is covered;
All the leaves from all the branches
Fall and fade and die and wither,
For I breathe, and lo! they are not.
From the waters and the marshes
Rise the wild goose and the heron,
Fly away to distant regions,
For I speak, and lo! they are not.
And where'er my footsteps wander,
All the wild beasts of the forest
Hide themselves in holes and caverns,
And the earth becomes as flintstone!"

"When I shake my flowing ringlets,"
Said the young man, softly laughing,
"Showers of rain fall warm and welcome,
Plants lift up their heads rejoicing,
Back unto their lakes and marshes
Come the wild goose and the heron,
Homeward shoots the arrowy swallow,
Sing the blue-bird and the robin,
And where'er my footsteps wander,
All the meadows wave with blossoms,
All the woodlands ring with music,
All the trees are dark with foliage!"

While they spake, the night departed;
From the distant realms of Wabun,
From his shining lodge of silver,
Like a warrior robed and painted,
Came the sun, and said: "Behold me!
Gheezis, the great sun, behold me!"

Then the old man's tongue was speechless,
And the air grew warm and pleasant,
And upon the wigwam sweetly
Sang the blue-bird and the robin,
And the stream began to murmur,
And a scent of growing grasses

Through the lodge was gently wafted.

And Segwun, the youthful stranger,
More distinctly in the daylight
Saw the icy face before him;
It was Peboan, the Winter!

From his eyes the tears were flowing,
As from melting lakes the streamlets,
And his body shrunk and dwindled
As the shouting sun ascended,
Till into the air it faded,
Till into the ground it vanished,
And the young man saw before him,
On the hearth-stone of the wigwam,
Where the fire had smoked and smouldered,
Saw the earliest flower of Spring-time,
Saw the Beauty of the Spring-time,
Saw the Miskodeed in blossom.

Thus it was that in the Northland
After that unheard-of coldness,
That intolerable Winter,
Came the Spring with all its splendor,
All its birds and all its blossoms,
All its flowers and leaves and grasses.

Sailing on the wind to northward,

Flying in great flocks, like arrows,
Like huge arrows shot through heaven,
Passed the swan, the Mahnahbezee,
Speaking almost as a man speaks;
And in long lines waving, bending
Like a bow-string snapped asunder,
The white goose, the Waw-be-wawa;
And in pairs, or singly flying,
Mahng the loon, with clangorous pinions,
The blue heron, the Shuh-shuh-gah,
And the growse, the Mushkodasa.

In the thickets and the meadows
Piped the blue-bird, the Owaissa,
On the summit of the lodges
Sang the Opechee, the robin,
In the covert of the pine-trees
Cooed the pigeon, the Omeme,
And the sorrowing Hiawatha,
Speechless in his infinite sorrow,
Heard their voices calling to him,
Went forth from his gloomy doorway,
Stood and gazed into the heaven,
Gazed upon the earth and waters.

From his wanderings far to eastward,

From the regions of the morning,
From the shining land of Wabun,
Homeward now returned Iagoo,
The great traveller, the great boaster,
Full of new and strange adventures,
Marvels many and many wonders.

And the people of the village
Listened to him as he told them
Of his marvellous adventures,
Laughing answered him in this wise:
"Ugh! it is indeed Iagoo!
No one else beholds such wonders!"

He had seen, he said, a water
Bigger than the Big-Sea-Water,
Broader than the Gitche Gumee,
Bitter so that none could drink it!
At each other looked the warriors,
Looked the women at each other,
Smiled, and said: "It cannot be so!
Kaw!" they said, "it cannot be so!"

O'er it, said he, o'er this water
Came a great canoe with pinions,
A canoe with wings came flying,
Bigger than a grove of pine-trees,

Taller than the tallest tree-tops!
And the old men and the women
Looked and tittered at each other;
"Kaw!" they said, "we don't believe it!"

From its mouth, he said, to greet him,
Came Waywassimo, the lightning,
Came the thunder, Annemeekee!
And the warriors and the women
Laughed aloud at poor Iagoo;
"Kaw!" they said, "what tales you tell us!"

In it, said he, came a people,
In the great canoe with pinions
Came, he said, a hundred warriors;
Painted white were all their faces,
And with hair their chins were covered!
And the warriors and the women
Laughed and shouted in derision,
Like the ravens on the tree-tops,
Like the crows upon the hemlocks.
"Kaw!" they said, "what lies you tell us!
Do not think that we believe them!"

Only Hiawatha laughed not,
But he gravely spake and answered
To their jeering and their jesting:

"True is all Iagoo tells us;
I have seen it in a vision,
Seen the great canoe with pinions,
Seen the people with white faces,
Seen the coming of this bearded
People of the wooden vessel
From the regions of the morning,
From the shining land of Wabun.

"Gitche Manito the Mighty,
The Great Spirit, the Creator,
Sends them hither on his errand,
Sends them to us with his message.
Wheresoe'er they move, before them
Swarms the stinging fly, the Ahmo,
Swarms the bee, the honey-maker;
Wheresoe'er they tread, beneath them
Springs a flower unknown among us,
Springs the White-man's Foot in blossom.

"Let us welcome, then, the strangers,
Hail them as our friends and brothers,
And the heart's right hand of friendship
Give them when they come to see us.
Gitche Manito, the Mighty,
Said this to me in my vision.

"I beheld, too, in that vision
All the secrets of the future,
Of the distant days that shall be.
I beheld the westward marches
Of the unknown, crowded nations.
All the land was full of people,
Restless, struggling, toiling, striving,
Speaking many tongues, yet feeling
But one heart-beat in their bosoms.
In the woodlands rang their axes,
Smoked their towns in all the valleys,
Over all the lakes and rivers
Rushed their great canoes of thunder.

"Then a darker, drearier vision
Passed before me, vague and cloud-like;
I beheld our nations scattered,
All forgetful of my counsels,
Weakened, warring with each other;
Saw the remnants of our people
Sweeping westward, wild and woful,
Like the cloud-rack of a tempest,
Like the withered leaves of autumn!"

## XXII.

### HIAWATHA'S DEPARTURE.

By the shore of Gitche Gumee,
By the shining Big-Sea-Water,
At the doorway of his wigwam,
In the pleasant Summer morning,
Hiawatha stood and waited.

All the air was full of freshness,
All the earth was bright and joyous,
And before him, through the sunshine,
Westward toward the neighboring forest
Passed in golden swarms the Ahmo
Passed the bees, the honey-makers,
Burning, singing in the sunshine.

Bright above him shone the heavens,
Level spread the lake before him;
From its bosom leaped the sturgeon,
Sparkling, flashing in the sunshine;

On its margin the great forest
Stood reflected in the water,
Every tree-top had its shadow,
Motionless beneath the water.

From the brow of Hiawatha
Gone was every trace of sorrow,
As the fog from off the water,
As the mist from off the meadow.
With a smile of joy and triumph,
With a look of exultation,
As of one who in a vision
Sees what is to be, but is not,
Stood and waited Hiawatha.

Toward the sun his hands were lifted,
Both the palms spread out against it,
And between the parted fingers
Fell the sunshine on his features,
Flecked with light his naked shoulders,
As it falls and flecks an oak-tree
Through the rifted leaves and branches.

O'er the water floating, flying,
Something in the hazy distance,
Something in the mists of morning,
Loomed and lifted from the water,

Now seemed floating, now seemed flying,
Coming nearer, nearer, nearer.

Was it Shingebis the diver?
Was it the pelican, the Shada?
Or the heron, the Shuh-shuh-gah?
Or the white goose, Waw-be-wawa,
With the water dripping, flashing
From its glossy neck and feathers?

It was neither goose nor diver,
Neither pelican nor heron,
O'er the water floating, flying,
Through the shining mist of morning,
But a birch canoe with paddles,
Rising, sinking on the water,
Dripping, flashing in the sunshine,
And within it came a people
From the distant land of Wabun,
From the farthest realms of morning
Came the Black-Robe chief, the Prophet,
He the Priest of Prayer, the Pale-face,
With his guides and his companions.

And the noble Hiawatha,
With his hands aloft extended,
Held aloft in sign of welcome,

Waited, full of exultation,
Till the birch canoe with paddles
Grated on the shining pebbles,
Stranded on the sandy margin,
Till the Black-Robe chief, the Pale-face,
With the cross upon his bosom,
Landed on the sandy margin.

   Then the joyous Hiawatha
Cried aloud and spake in this wise:
"Beautiful is the sun, O strangers,
When you come so far to see us!
All our town in peace awaits you,
All our doors stand open for you;
You shall enter all our wigwams,
For the heart's right hand we give you.

   "Never bloomed the earth so gayly,
Never shone the sun so brightly,
As to-day they shine and blossom
When you come so far to see us!
Never was our lake so tranquil,
Nor so free from rocks and sand-bars;
For your birch canoe in passing
Has removed both rock and sand-bar!

   "Never before had our tobacco

Such a sweet and pleasant flavor,
Never the broad leaves of our corn-fields
Were so beautiful to look on,
As they seem to us this morning,
When you come so far to see us!"

And the Black-Robe chief made answer,
Stammered in his speech a little,
Speaking words yet unfamiliar:
"Peace be with you, Hiawatha,
Peace be with you and your people,
Peace of prayer, and peace of pardon,
Peace of Christ, and joy of Mary!"

Then the generous Hiawatha
Led the strangers to his wigwam,
Seated them on skins of bison,
Seated them on skins of ermine,
And the careful, old Nokomis
Brought them food in bowls of bass-wood,
Water brought in birchen dippers,
And the calumet, the peace-pipe,
Filled and lighted for their smoking.

All the old men of the village,
All the warriors of the nation,
All the Jossakeeds, the prophets,

The magicians, the Wabenos,
And the medicine-men, the Medas,
Came to bid the strangers welcome;
"It is well," they said, "O brothers,
That you come so far to see us!"

In a circle round the doorway,
With their pipes they sat in silence,
Waiting to behold the strangers,
Waiting to receive their message;
Till the Black-Robe chief, the Pale-face,
From the wigwam came to greet them,
Stammering in his speech a little,
Speaking words yet unfamiliar;
"It is well," they said, "O brother,
That you come so far to see us!"

Then the Black-Robe chief, the prophet,
Told his message to the people,
Told the purport of his mission,
Told them of the Virgin Mary,
And her blessed Son, the Saviour,
How in distant lands and ages
He had lived on earth as we do;
How he fasted, prayed, and labored;
How the Jews, the tribe accursed,

Mocked him, scourged him, crucified him;
How he rose from where they laid him,
Walked again with his disciples,
And ascended into heaven.

And the chiefs made answer, saying:
"We have listened to your message,
We have heard your words of wisdom,
We will think on what you tell us.
It is well for us, O brothers,
That you come so far to see us!"

Then they rose up and departed
Each one homeward to his wigwam,
To the young men and the women
Told the story of the strangers
Whom the Master of Life had sent them
From the shining land of Wabun.

Heavy with the heat and silence
Grew the afternoon of Summer;
With a drowsy sound the forest
Whispered round the sultry wigwam,
With a sound of sleep the water
Rippled on the beach below it;
From the corn-fields shrill and ceaseless
Sang the grasshopper, Pah-puk-keena:

And the guests of Hiawatha,
Weary with the heat of Summer,
Slumbered in the sultry wigwam.

Slowly o'er the simmering landscape
Fell the evening's dusk and coolness,
And the long and level sunbeams
Shot their spears into the forest,
Breaking through its shields of shadow,
Rushed into each secret ambush,
Searched each thicket, dingle, hollow;
Still the guests of Hiawatha
Slumbered in the silent wigwam.

From his place rose Hiawatha,
Bade farewell to old Nokomis,
Spake in whispers, spake in this wise,
Did not wake the guests, that slumbered:
"I am going, O Nokomis,
On a long and distant journey,
To the portals of the Sunset,
To the regions of the home-wind,
Of the Northwest wind, Keewaydin.
But these guests I leave behind me,
In your watch and ward I leave them;
See that never harm comes near them,

See that never fear molests them,
Never danger nor suspicion,
Never want of food or shelter,
In the lodge of Hiawatha!"

Forth into the village went he,
Bade farewell to all the warriors,
Bade farewell to all the young men,
Spake persuading, spake in this wise:

"I am going, O my people,
On a long and distant journey;
Many moons and many winters
Will have come, and will have vanished,
Ere I come again to see you.
But my guests I leave behind me;
Listen to their words of wisdom,
Listen to the truth they tell you,
For the Master of Life has sent them
From the land of light and morning!"

On the shore stood Hiawatha,
Turned and waved his hand at parting;
On the clear and luminous water
Launched his birch canoe for sailing,
From the pebbles of the margin
Shoved it forth into the water;

Whispered to it, "Westward! westward!"
And with speed it darted forward.

And the evening sun descending
Set the clouds on fire with redness,
Burned the broad sky, like a prairie,
Left upon the level water
One long track and trail of splendor,
Down whose stream, as down a river,
Westward, westward Hiawatha
Sailed into the fiery sunset,
Sailed into the purple vapors,
Sailed into the dusk of evening.

And the people from the margin
Watched him floating, rising, sinking,
Till the birch canoe seemed lifted
High into that sea of splendor,
Till it sank into the vapors
Like the new moon slowly, slowly
Sinking in the purple distance.

And they said: "Farewell for ever!"
Said, "Farewell, O Hiawatha!"
And the forests, dark and lonely,
Moved through all their depths of darkness,
Sighed: "Farewell, O Hiawatha!"

And the waves upon the margin
Rising, rippling on the pebbles,
Sobbed: "Farewell, O Hiawatha!"
And the heron, the Shuh-shuh-gah,
From her haunts among the fen-lands,
Screamed: "Farewell, O Hiawatha!"
   Thus departed Hiawatha,
Hiawatha the Beloved,
In the glory of the sunset,
In the purple mists of evening,
To the regions of the home-wind,
Of the Northwest wind Keewaydin,
To the Islands of the Blessed,
To the kingdom of Ponemah,
To the land of the Hereafter!

# GLOSSARY.

Adjidau'mo, *the red squirrel.*

Ahdeek', *the reindeer.*

Ahkose'win, *fever.*

Ahmeek', *the beaver.*

Ah'mo, *the bee.*

Algon'quin, *Ojibway.*

Annemee'kee, *the thunder.*

Apuk'wa, *a bulrush.*

Baim-wa'wa, *the sound of the thunder.*

Bemah'gut, *the grape-vine.*

Be'na, *the pheasant.*

Big-Sea-Water, *Lake Superior.*

Bukada'win, *famine.*

Cheemaun', *a birch canoe.*

Chetowaik', *the plover.*

Chibia'bos, *a musician; friend of Hiawatha; ruler in the Land of Spirits.*

Dahin'da, *the bull-frog.*

Dush-kwo-ne'-she, *or* Kwo-ne'-she, *the dragon-fly.*

Esa, *shame upon you.*

Ewa-yea', *lullaby.*

Ghee'zis, *the sun.*

Gitche Gu'mee, *the Big-Sea-Water, Lake Superior.*

Gitche Man'ito, *the Great Spirit, the Master of Life.*

Gushkewau', *the darkness.*

Hiawa'tha, *the Wise Man, the Teacher; son of Mudjekeewis, the West-Wind, and Wenonah, daughter of Nokomis.*

Ia'goo, *a great boaster and story-teller.*

Inin'ewug, *men, or pawns in the Game of the Bowl, Wedgemen.*

Ishkoodah', *fire; a comet.*

Jee'bi, *a ghost, a spirit.*

Joss'akeed, *a prophet.*

Ka'beyun, *the West-Wind.*

Kabibonok'ka, *the North-Wind.*

Kagh, *the hedgehog.*

Ka'go, *do not.*

Kahgahgee', *the raven.*

Kaw, *no.*

Kaween', *no indeed.*

Kayoshk', *the sea-gull.*

Kee'go, *a fish.*

Keeway'din, *the Northwest wind, the Home-wind.*

Kena'beek, *a serpent.*

Keneu', *the great war-eagle.*

Keno'zha, *the pickerel.*

Ko'ko-ko'ho, *the owl.*

Kuntassoo', *the Game of Plum-stones.*

247

Kwa'sind, *the Strong Man.*

Kwo-ne'-she, *or* Dush-kwo-ne'she, *the dragon-fly.*

Mahnahbe'zee, *the swan.*

Mahng, *the loon.*

Mahn-go-tay'see, *loon-hearted, brave.*

Mahnomo'nee, *wild rice.*

Ma'ma, *the woodpecker.*

Man'ito, *spirit.*

Maskeno'zha, *the pike.*

Me'da, *a medicine-man.*

Me'damin, *the art of healing.*

Meenah'ga, *the blueberry.*

Megissog'won, *the great Pearl-Feather, a magician, and the Manito of Wealth.*

Meshinau'wa, *a pipe-bearer.*

Minjekah'wun, *Hiawatha's mittens.*

Minneha'ha, *Laughing Water; a water-fall on a stream running into the Mississippi, between Fort Snelling and the Falls of St. Anthony.*

Minneha'ha, *Laughing Water; wife of Hiawatha.*

Minne-wa'wa, *a pleasant sound, as of the wind in the trees.*

Mishe-Mo'kwa, *the Great Bear.*

Mishe-Nah'ma, *the Great Sturgeon.*

Miskodeed', *the Spring-Beauty, the Claytonia Virginica.*

Mitche Manito, *spirit of evil.*

Monda'min, *maize; Indian corn.*

Moon of Bright Nights, *April.*

Moon of Leaves, *May.*

Moon of Strawberries, *June.*

Moon of the Falling Leaves, *September.*

Moon of Snow-shoes, *November*

Mudjekee'wis, *the West-Wind; father of Hiawatha.*

Mudway-aush'ka, *sound of waves on a shore.*

Mushkoda'sa, *the grouse.*

Mus'koday, *the meadow.*

Nah'ma, *the sturgeon.*

Nah'ma-wusk, *spearmint.*

Na'gow Wudj'oo, *the Sand Dunes of Lake Superior.*

Nawada'ha, *a sweet singer.*

Nee-ba-naw'-baigs, *water-spirits.*

Nenemoo'sha, *sweetheart.*

Nepah'win, *spirit of sleep.*

Noko'mis, *a grandmother; mother of Wenonah.*

No'sa, *my father.*

Nush'ka, *look! look!*

Odah'min, *the strawberry.*

Ojeeg', *the summer-water, the Fisher Weasel.*

Okahah'wis, *the fresh-water herring.*

Ome'me, *the pigeon.*

Ona'gon, *a bowl.*

Onaway', *awake.*

Ope'chee, *the robin.*

Osse'o, *Son of the Evening Star.*

Owais'sa, *the blue-bird.*

Oweenee', *wife of Osseo.*

Ozawa'beek, *a round piece of brass or copper in the Game of the Bowl.*

Pah-puk-kee'na, *the grasshopper.*

Paimosaid', *the stealthy walker, thief.*

Pau'guk, *death.*

Pau-Puk-Kee'wis, *the handsome Yenadizze, the Storm Fool.*

Pauwa'ting, *Saut Sainte Marie.*

# GLOSSARY.

Pe'boan, *Winter.*

Pem'ican, *meat of the deer or buffalo dried and pounded.*

Pezhekee', *the bison.*

Pishnekuh', *the brant.*

Pone'mah, *hereafter.*

Pugasaing', *Game of the Bowl.*

Pugamau'gun, *a war-club.*

Pukwana, *smoke of the Peace Pipe.*

Puk-Wudj'ies, *little wild men of the woods; pigmies.*

Sah-sah-je'-wun, *rapids.*

Sah'wa, *the perch.*

Sebowish'a, *a rivulet, brook.*

Segwun', *Spring.*

Sha'da, *the pelican.*

Shahbo'min, *the gooseberry.*

Shah'-shah, *long ago.*

Shaugoda'ya, *a coward.*

Shawgashee', *the craw-fish.*

Shawonda'see, *the South-Wind.*

Shaw-shaw, *the swallow.*

Shesh'ebwug, *ducks; pieces in the Game of the Bowl.*

Shin'gebis, *the diver, or grebe.*

Showain'neme'shin, *pity me.*

Shuh-shuh'-gah, *the blue heron.*

Soan-ge-ta'ha, *strong-hearted.*

Subbeka'she, *the spider.*

Sugge'ma, *the mosquito.*

Tam'arack, *the larch-tree.*

Tawasen'tha, *Norman's Kill, Albany County, New York.*

To'tem, *family coat-of-arms.*

Ugh, *yes.*

Ugudwash', *the sun-fish.*

Unktahee', *the god of water.*

Wabas'so, *the rabbit; the North.*

Wabe'no, *a magician, a juggler.*

Wabe'no-wusk, *yarrow.*

Wa'bun, *the East-Wind.*

Wa'bun An'nung, *the Star of the East, the Morning Star.*

Wa'gemin, *crooked grain, thief of cornfields.*

Wahono'win, *a cry of lamentation.*

Wah-wah-tay'see, *the fire-fly.*

Wam'pum, *beads of shell.*

Waubewy'on, *a white skin wrapper.*

Wa'wa, *the wild-goose.*

Waw'beek, *a rock.*

Waw-be-wa'wa, *the white goose.*

Wawonais'sa, *the whippoorwill.*

Way-muk-kwa'na, *the caterpillar.*

Wen'digoes, *giants.*

Weno'nah, *Hiawatha's mother, daughter of Nokomis.*

Yenadiz'ze, *an idler and gambler; an Indian dandy.*

# NOTES.

THE SONG OF HIAWATHA. — This Indian Edda — if I
may so call it — is founded on a tradition prevalent among
the North American Indians, of a personage of miraculous birth, who was sent among them to clear their rivers,
forests, and fishing-grounds, and to teach them the arts of
peace. He was known among different tribes by the several names of Michabou, Chiabo, Manabozo, Tarenyawa-
gon, and Hiawatha. Mr. Schoolcraft gives an account of
him in his *Algic Researches*, Vol. I., p. 134 [*see* Appen-
dix]; and in his *History, Condition, and Prospects of the
Indian Tribes of the United States*, Part III., p. 314, may
be found the Iroquois form of the tradition, derived from
the verbal narrations of an Onondaga chief.

Into this old tradition I have woven other curious
Indian legends, drawn chiefly from the various and valu-
able writings of Mr. Schoolcraft, to whom the literary
world is greatly indebted for his indefatigable zeal in res-
cuing from oblivion so much of the legendary lore of the
Indians.

The scene of the poem is among the Ojibways on the
southern shore of Lake Superior, in the region between
the Pictured Rocks and the Grand Sable.

Page 3. *In the Vale of Tawasentha.*

This valley, now called Norman's Kill, is in Albany County, New York.

Page 7. *On the Mountains of the Prairie.*

Mr. Catlin, in his *Letters and Notes on the Manners, Customs, and Condition of the North American Indians,* Vol. II., p. 160, gives an interesting account of the *Côteau des Prairies,* and the Red Pipe-stone Quarry. He says:—

"Here (according to their traditions) happened the mysterious birth of the red pipe, which has blown its fumes of peace and war to the remotest corners of the continent; which has visited every warrior, and passed through its reddened stem the irrevocable oath of war and desolation. And here also the peace-breathing calumet was born, and fringed with the eagle's quills, which has shed its thrilling fumes over the land, and soothed the fury of the relentless savage.

"The Great Spirit at an ancient period here called the Indian nations together, and standing on the precipice of the red pipe-stone rock, broke from its wall a piece, and made a huge pipe by turning it in his hand, which he smoked over them, and to the North, the South, the East, and the West, and told them that this stone was red, — that it was their flesh, — that they must use it for their pipes of peace, — that it belonged to them all, and that the war-club and scalping-knife must not be raised on its ground. At the last whiff of his pipe his head went into a great cloud, and the whole surface of the rock for several miles was melted and glazed; two great ovens were opened beneath, and two women (guardian spirits of the place) entered them in a blaze of fire; and they are heard there yet (Tso-mec-cos-tee and Tso-me-cos-te-won-dee), answering to the invocations of the high-priests or medicine-men, who consult them when they are visitors to this sacred place."

Page 17.   *Hark you, Bear! you are a coward.*

This anecdote is from Heckewelder.   In his account of the *Indian Nations*, he describes an Indian hunter as addressing a bear in nearly these words.   "I was present," he says, "at the delivery of this curious invective; when the hunter had despatched the bear, I asked him how he thought that poor animal could understand what he said to it?   'O,' said he in answer, 'the bear understood me very well; did you not observe how *ashamed* he looked while I was upbraiding him?'" — *Transactions of the American Philosophical Society*, Vol. I., p. 240.

Page 31.   *Hush! the Naked Bear will get thee!*

Heckewelder, in a letter published in the *Transactions of the American Philosophical Society*, Vol. IV., p. 260, speaks of this tradition as prevalent among the Mohicans and Delawares.

"Their reports," he says, "run thus : that among all animals that had been formerly in this country, this was the most ferocious; that it was much larger than the largest of the common bears, and remarkably long-bodied; all over (except a spot of hair on its back of a white color) naked. . . .

"The history of this animal used to be a subject of conversation among the Indians, especially when in the woods a hunting.   I have also heard them say to their children when crying : 'Hush! the naked bear will hear you, be upon you, and devour you.'"

Page 50.   *Where the Falls of Minnehaha, etc.*

"The scenery about Fort Snelling is rich in beauty. The Falls of St. Anthony are familiar to travellers, and to readers of Indian sketches. Between the fort and these falls are the 'Little Falls,' forty feet in height, on a stream that empties into the Mississippi. The Indians call them Mine-hah-hah, or 'laughing waters.' " — Mrs. Eastman's *Dacotah, or Legends of the Sioux,* Introduction, p. ii.

Page 122.   *Sand Hills of the Nagow Wudjoo!*

A description of the *Grand Sable,* or great sand dunes of Lake Superior, is given in Foster and Whitney's *Report on the Geology of the Lake Superior Land District,* Part II., p. 131.

"The Grand Sable possesses a scenic interest little inferior to that of the Pictured Rocks. The explorer passes abruptly from a coast of consolidated sand to one of loose materials ; and although in the one case the cliffs are less precipitous, yet in the other they attain a higher altitude. He sees before him a long reach of coast, resembling a vast sand-bank, more than three hundred and fifty feet in height, without a trace of vegetation. Ascending to the top, rounded hillocks of blown sand are observed, with occasional clumps of trees, standing out like oases in the desert."

Page 123.   *Onaway! Awake, beloved!*

The original of this song may be found in *Littell's Living Age,* Vol. XXV., p. 45.   *See* Appendix.

Page 128.   *Or the Red Swan floating, flying.*

The fanciful tradition of the Red Swan may be found in Schoolcraft's *Algic Researches,* Vol. II., p. 9.   Three brothers were hunting on a wager to see who would bring home the first game.

"They were to shoot no other animal," so the legend says, "but such as each was in the habit of killing." They set out different ways ; Odjibwa, the youngest, had not gone far before he saw a bear, an animal he was not to kill, by the agreement. He followed him close, and drove an arrow through him, which brought him to the ground. Although contrary to the bet, he immediately commenced skinning him, when suddenly something red tinged all the air around him. He rubbed his eyes, thinking he was perhaps deceived, but without effect, for the red hue continued. At length he heard a strange noise at a distance. It first appeared like a human voice; but after following the sound for some distance, he reached the shores of a lake, and soon saw the object he was looking for. At a distance out in the lake sat a most beautiful Red Swan, whose plumage glittered in the sun, and who would now and then make the same noise he had heard. He was within long bow-shot, and pulling the arrow from the bow-string up to his ear, took deliberate aim and shot. The arrow took no effect ; and he shot and shot again till his quiver was empty. Still the swan remained, moving round and round, stretching its long neck and dipping its bill into the water, as if heedless of the arrows shot at it. Odjibwa ran home, and got all his own and his brother's arrows, and shot them all away. He then stood and gazed at the beautiful bird. While standing, he remembered his brother's saying that in their deceased father's medicine-sack were three magic arrows. Off he started, his anxiety to kill the swan overcoming all scruples. At any other time he would have deemed it sacrilege to open his father's medicine-sack ; but now he hastily seized the three arrows and ran back, leaving the other contents of the sack scattered over the lodge. The swan was still there. He shot the first arrow with great precision, and came very near to it. The second came still closer ; as he took the last arrow, he felt his arm firmer, and drawing it up with vigor, saw it pass through the neck of the swan a little above the breast. Still it did not prevent the bird from flying off, which it did, however, at first slowly, flapping its wings and rising gradually into the air, and then flying off toward the sinking of the sun." — Pp. 10–12.

Page 143.   *When I think of my beloved.*

The original of this song may be found in *Oneóta*, p. 15.

Page 144.   *Sing the mysteries of Mondamin.*

The Indians hold the maize, or Indian corn, in great veneration. "They esteem it so important and divine a grain," says Schoolcraft, "that their story-tellers invented various tales, in which this idea is symbolized under the form of a special gift from the Great Spirit. The Odjibwa-Algonquins, who call it Mon-dá-min, that is, the Spirit's grain or berry, have a pretty story of this kind, in which the stalk in full tassel is represented as descending from the sky, under the guise of a handsome youth, in answer to the prayers of a young man at his fast of virility, or coming to manhood.

"It is well known that corn-planting and corn-gathering, at least among all the still *uncolonized* tribes, are left entirely to the females and children, and a few superannuated old men. It is not generally known, perhaps, that this labor is not compulsory, and that it is assumed by the females as a just equivalent, in their view, for the onerous and continuous labor of the other sex, in providing meats and skins for clothing by the chase, and in defending their villages against their enemies, and keeping intruders off their territories. A good Indian housewife deems this a part of her prerogative, and prides herself to have a store of corn to exercise her hospitality, or duly honor her husband's hospitality, in the entertainment of the lodge guests." — *Oneóta*, p. 82.

Page 146.  *Thus the fields shall be more fruitful.*

"A singular proof of this belief, in both sexes, of the mysterious influence of the steps of a woman on the vegetable and insect creation, is found in an ancient custom, which was related to me, respecting corn-planting. It was the practice of the hunter's wife, when the field of corn had been planted, to choose the first dark or over-clouded evening to perform a secret circuit, *sans habillement*, around the field. For this purpose she slipped out of the lodge in the evening, unobserved, to some obscure nook, where she completely disrobed. Then, taking her matchecota, or principal garment, in one hand, she dragged it around the field. This was thought to insure a prolific crop, and to prevent the assaults of insects and worms upon the grain. It was supposed they could not creep over the charmed line." — *Oneóta*, p. 83.

Page 150.  *With his prisoner-string he bound him.*

"These cords," says Mr. Tanner, "are made of the bark of the elm-tree, by boiling and then immersing it in cold water. . . . The leader of a war party commonly carries several fastened about his waist; and if, in the course of the fight, any one of his young men takes a prisoner, it is his duty to bring him immediately to the chief, to be tied, and the latter is responsible for his safe-keeping." — *Narrative of Captivity and Adventures,* p. 412.

Page 153.   *Wagemin, the thief of corn-fields!*
            *Paimosaid, the skulking robber!*

"If one of the young female huskers finds a *red* ear of corn, it is typical of a brave admirer, and is regarded as a fitting present to some young warrior.  But if the ear be *crooked*, and tapering to a point, no matter what color, the whole circle is set in a roar, and *wa-ge-min* is the word shouted aloud.  It is the symbol of a thief in the corn-field.  It is considered as the image of an old man stooping as he enters the lot.  Had the chisel of Praxiteles been employed to produce this image, it could not more vividly bring to the minds of the merry group the idea of a pilferer of their favorite mondámin. . . .

"The literal meaning of the term is a mass, or crooked ear of grain ; but the ear of corn so called is a conventional type of a little old man pilfering ears of corn in a corn-field.  It is in this manner that a single word or term, in these curious languages, becomes the fruitful parent of many ideas.  And we can thus perceive why it is that the word *wagemin* is alone competent to excite merriment in the husking circle.

"This term is taken as the basis of the cereal chorus, or corn song, as sung by the Northern Algonquin tribes.  It is coupled with the phrase *Paimosaid,* — a permutative form of the Indian substantive, made from the verb *pim-o-sa,* to walk.  Its literal meaning is, *he who walks,* or *the walker ;* but the ideas conveyed by it are, he who walks

by night to pilfer corn. It offers, therefore, a kind of par-
allelism in expression to the preceding term." — *Oneóta,*
p. 254.

Page 176.     *Pugasaing, with thirteen pieces.*

This Game of the Bowl is the principal game of hazard
among the Northern tribes of Indians. Mr. Schoolcraft
gives a particular account of it in *Oneóta,* p. 85. "This
game," he says, "is very fascinating to some portions of
the Indians. They stake at it their ornaments, weapons,
clothing, canoes, horses, everything in fact they possess ;
and have been known, it is said, to set up their wives and
children, and even to forfeit their own liberty. Of such
desperate stakes I have seen no examples, nor do I think
the game itself in common use. It is rather confined to
certain persons, who hold the relative rank of gamblers in
Indian society, — men who are not noted as hunters or
warriors, or steady providers for their families. Among
these are persons who bear the term of *Ienadizze-wug,*
that is, wanderers about the country, braggadocios, or
fops. It can hardly be classed with the popular games of
amusement, by which skill and dexterity are acquired. I
have generally found the chiefs and graver men of the
tribes, who encouraged the young men to play ball, and
are sure to be present at the customary sports, to witness
and sanction and applaud them, speak lightly and dis-
paragingly of this game of hazard. Yet it cannot be
denied that some of the chiefs, distinguished in war and
the chase at the West, can be referred to as lending their
example to its fascinating power."

See also his *History, Condition, and Prospects of the
Indian Tribes,* Part II., p. 72.

Page 197.   *To the Pictured Rocks of sandstone.*

The reader will find a long description of the Pictured Rocks in Foster and Whitney's *Report on the Geology of the Lake Superior Land District*, Part II., p. 124. From this I make the following extract: —

"The Pictured Rocks may be described, in general terms, as a series of sandstone bluffs extending along the shore of Lake Superior for about five miles, and rising, in most places, vertically from the water, without any beach at the base, to a height varying from fifty to nearly two hundred feet. Were they simply a line of cliffs, they might not, so far as relates to height or extent, be worthy of a rank among great natural curiosities, although such an assemblage of rocky strata, washed by the waves of the great lake, would not, under any circumstances, be destitute of grandeur. To the voyager coasting along their base in his frail canoe, they would at all times be an object of dread; the recoil of the surf, the rock-bound coast, affording for miles no place of refuge, the lowering sky, the rising wind, all these would excite his apprehension, and induce him to ply a vigorous oar until the dreaded wall was passed. But in the Pictured Rocks there are two features which communicate to the scenery a wonderful and almost unique character. These are, first, the curious manner in which the cliffs have been excavated and worn away by the action of the lake, which for centuries has dashed an ocean-like surf against their base; and second, the equally curious manner in which large portions of the surface have been colored by bands of brilliant hues.

"It is from the latter circumstance that the name by which these cliffs are known to the American traveller is derived ; while that applied to them by the French voy-ageurs ('Les Portails') is derived from the former, and by far the most striking peculiarity.

"The term *Pictured Rocks* has been in use for a great length of time ; but when it was first applied we have been unable to discover. It would seem that the first travellers were more impressed with the novel and strik-ing distribution of colors on the surface than with the astonishing variety of form into which the cliffs them-selves have been worn. . . .

"Our voyageurs had many legends to relate of the pranks of the *Menni-bojou* in these caverns, and in answer to our inquiries, seemed disposed to fabricate stories without end of the achievements of this Indian deity."

Page 236. *Toward the sun his hands were lifted.*

In this manner, and with such salutations, was Father Marquette received by the Illinois. See his *Voyages et Découvertes*, Section V.

# APPENDIX.

### ILLUSTRATIVE SELECTIONS FROM SCHOOLCRAFT.

*Showing the sources from which Longfellow took materials for Hiawatha.*

HENRY R. SCHOOLCRAFT, in his great but ill-digested compilation on the American Indians, gives the following account of Manabozho: —

"At a certain time a great Manito came on earth, and took a wife of men. She had four sons at a birth, and died in ushering them into the world. The first was Manabozho, who is the friend of the human race. The second was Chibiabos,[1] who has the care of the dead, and presides over the country of souls. The third was Wabasso, who, as soon as he saw light, fled to the North, where he was changed into a white rabbit, and, under that name, is considered a great spirit. The fourth was Chokanipok, or the man of flint, or the fire-stone.

"Whenever the Algonkins gathered around the winter fire, they never wearied of repeating the story of Manabozho or Michabo, the Great Hare, of whom they spoke as their common ancestor, and the clan that bore his totem was looked up to with peculiar respect. He was the pa-

[1] Page 66.

tron and founder of the Meda worship, the inventor of
picture-writing, the father and guardian of their nation,
the ruler of the winds, even the maker and preserver of
the world, and the creator of the sun and moon. From
a grain of sand brought from the bottom of the primeval
ocean he fashioned the habitable land, and set it floating
on the waters. Manabozho appears in reality to have been
the personification of the purest conception the Indian
possessed concerning the Deity.

"The first thing Manabozho did when he grew up was
to go to war against Chokanipok, whom he accused of his
mother's death. The contests between them were fright-
ful and long-continued ; and wherever they had a combat,
the face of nature still shows signs of it. Fragments were
cut from Chokanipok's flesh, which were transformed into
stones; and Manabozho finally destroyed his antagonist by
tearing out his entrails, which were changed into vines.
All the flint-stones which are scattered over the earth were
produced this way, and they supplied men with the prin-
ciple of fire.

"Manabozho was the author of arts and improvements.
He taught men how to make agakwuts (axes), lances, and
arrow-points, and all implements of bone and stone, and
also how to make snares and traps and nets, to take animals and birds and fishes."

Hiawatha, on the other hand, — the name signifying
"surpassing all in wisdom," — though sometimes con-
fused with Manabozho, was a very different character. He
was known in the legend as "the mischief-maker," "the
impersonation of evil, the essential badness, combined with
low cunning, ineffable weakness, and the paltriest ambi-
tion ;" but in Indian history he is supposed, under the

name of Tarenyawagan, to have been a genuine character, who at the end of the seventeenth century, by his genius for organizing, welded the five nations into a sort of republic. De Costa, who felt called to improve on Longfellow's poem, says: —

"Essential republicanism in this country began with the League of the Five Nations, who were taught the advantages of the system by Hiawatha."

Mr. Schoolcraft in his *Algic Researches* [1] gives the following legends, which are interesting to read in connection with Longfellow's *Hiawatha*. They are somewhat condensed.

## SHAWONDASEE.

MUDJEKEWIS and nine [2] brothers conquered the Mammoth Bear, and obtained the Sacred Belt of Wampum, the great means of happiness to men. The chief honor of this achievement was awarded to Mudjekewis, the youngest of the ten, who received the government of the West Winds. He is therefore called Kabeyun, the father of the Winds. To his son Wabun, he gave the East; to Shawondasee the South, and to Kabibonokka the North.

Shawondasee is represented as an affluent, plethoric old man, who has grown unwieldy from repletion, and seldom moves. He keeps his eyes steadily fixed on the North. When he sighs in autumn, we have those balmy southern airs which communicate warmth and delight on the northern hemisphere, and make the Indian Summer.

---

[1] *Algic Researches, Comprising Inquiries Respecting the Mental Characteristics of the North American Indians.* HENRY ROWE SCHOOLCRAFT. New York, 1839.

[2] Page 1c.

One day, while gazing toward the North, he beheld a beautiful young woman of slender and majestic form standing on the plains.[1] She appeared in the same place for several days ; but what most attracted his admiration was her bright and flowing locks of yellow hair. Ever dilatory, however, he contented himself with gazing. At length he saw, or fancied he saw, her head enveloped in a pure white mass like snow. This excited his jealousy toward his brother Kabibonokka, and he threw out a succession of short and rapid sighs, when lo! the air was filled with light filaments of a silvery hue, but the object of his affections had forever vanished.

In reality the southern airs had blown off the fine winged seed-vessels of the prairie dandelion.

## MANABOZHO.

THE accounts which the Indians hand down of a remarkable personage of miraculous birth, who waged a warfare with monsters, performed the most extravagant and heroic feats, underwent a catastrophe like Jonah's, and survived a general deluge, constitute a very prominent portion of their cabin lore. Whatever man could do, he could do. He affected all the powers of a necromancer. He wielded the arts of a demon, and had the ubiquity of a god. He leaps over extensive regions of country like an *ignis fatuus*. He appears suddenly like an avatar, or saunters over weary wastes a poor and starving hunter. His voice is at one moment deep and sonorous as a thunder-clap, and at another clothed with the softness of

[1] Page 25.

feminine supplication. His birth and parentage are obscure. Story says his grandmother was the daughter of the moon. Having been married but a short time, her rival attracted her to a grape-vine swing on the banks of a lake, and by one bold exertion pitched her into its centre, from which she fell through to the earth.[1] Having a daughter, the fruit of her lunar marriage, she was very careful in instructing her, from early infancy, to beware of the west wind, and never, in stooping, to expose herself to its influence.[2] In some unguarded moment the precaution was neglected. In an instant the gale, invading her robes, scattered them upon its wings, and accomplishing its Tarquinic purpose, at the same moment annihilated her. At the scene of this catastrophe her mother found a fœtus-like mass, which she carefully and tenderly nursed, till it assumed the beautiful and striking lineaments of the infant Manabozho.[3]

He soon evinced the sagacity, cunning, perseverance, and heroic courage which constitute the admiration of the Indians. And he relied largely on these in the gratification of an ambitious, vain-glorious, and mischief-loving disposition. In wisdom and energy he was superior to any one who had ever lived before. Yet he was simple when circumstances required it, and was ever the object of tricks and ridicule in others. He could transform himself into any animal he pleased, bring war or manito, as circumstances rendered necessary. He often conversed with animals, fowls, reptiles, and fishes.[4] He deemed himself related to them, and invariably addressed them by the term, "My brother;" and one of his greatest resources, when hard pressed, was to change himself into their shapes.

[1] Page 28.    [2] Page 29.    [3] Page 30.    [4] Page 34.

## MANABOZHO AND HIS FATHER.[1]

MANABOZHO was living with his grandmother near the edge of a wide prairie. While there he thought to himself, "It is singular that I am so simple, and my grandmother so wise, and that I have neither father nor mother. I have never heard a word about them. I must ask and find out."

He went home, and sat down silent and dejected. At length his grandmother asked him, —

"Manabozho, what is the matter with you?"

He answered, "I wish you would tell me whether I have any parents living, and who my relations are."

"Yes," she said; "you have a father and three brothers living. Your mother is dead. She was taken without the consent of her parents by your father, the West. Your brothers are the North, East, and South; and, being older than yourself, your father has given them great power with the winds, according to their names. You are the youngest of his children. Your mother died in giving you birth, owing to the ill-treatment of your father."

He appeared to be rejoiced to hear that his father was living, for he had already thought in his heart to try to kill him.

He told his grandmother he should set out in the morning to visit him. She said it was a long distance to the place where Ningabiun lived. He set out, and soon reached the place; for every step he took covered a large surface of ground. The meeting took place on a high mountain in the West. His father was very happy to see him. He also appeared pleased. They spent some days in talking

[1] Canto IV.

with each other. One evening Manabozho asked his father what he was most afraid of on earth. He replied, —

"Nothing."

"But is there not something you dread here? Tell me?"

At last his father said, yielding, —

"Yes, there is a black stone found in such a place.[1] It is the only thing earthly I am afraid of ; for if it should hit me on any part of my body it would injure me very much."

He said this as a secret, and in return asked his son the same question. Knowing each other's power, although the son's was limited, the father feared him on account of his great strength. Manabozho answered, "Nothing," intending to avoid the question, or to refer to some harmless object as of the one of which he was afraid. He was asked again and again, and answered, "Nothing." But the West said, —

"There must be something you are afraid of."

"Well, I will tell you what it is." But before he would pronounce the word, he affected great dread.

The West told him to banish his fears. At last he cried out, —

"It is the root of the *apukwa*, the bulrush." He appeared to be exhausted by the effort of pronouncing the word, in all this skilfully acting a studied part. Some time after he observed, —

"I will get some of the black rock."

The West said, —

"Far be it from you ; do not do so, my son."

He still persisted.

"Well," said the father, "I will also get the *apukwa* root."

Manabozho immediately cried out, "*Kago! kago!*"[1]—
do not! do not! — affecting, as before, to be in great dread
of it, but really wishing, by this course, to urge on the
West to procure it, that he might draw him into the combat. He went out and got a large piece of the black rock,
and brought it home. The West also took care to bring
the dreaded root.

He asked his father whether he had been the cause of
his mother's death.

The answer was, "Yes."

He then took up the rock and struck him. Blow led
to blow, and then commenced an obstinate and furious
combat which continued several days. Fragments of the
rock broken off under Manabozho's blows can be seen in
various places to this day.

The West was forced to give ground. Manabozho
drove him across rivers and over mountains and lakes,
and at last he came to the brink of the world.

"Hold!" cried he; "my son, you know my power,[2]
and that it is impossible to kill me. Desist, and I will
also portion you out with as much power as your brothers.
The four quarters of the world are already occupied; but
you can go and do a great deal of good to the people of
the earth, which is infested with large serpents (*genabeeks*), beasts, and monsters (*weendigon*), who make great
havoc among the inhabitants. Go, and do good. You
have the power now to do so, and your fame with the
kings of this earth will last forever. When you have finished your work, I will have a place provided for you.
You will then go and sit with your brother Kabibonokka
in the north."

[1] Page 45.    [2] Page 48.

Manabozho was pacified. He returned to his lodge, where he was confined by the wounds he had received. But from his grandmother's skill in medicines he was soon recovered.


## MON-DAW-MIN, OR THE ORIGIN OF MAIZE.[1]

In times past a poor Indian was living with his wife and children in a beautiful part of the country. He was not only poor, but inexpert in procuring food for his family, and his children were all too young to give him assistance. Although poor, he was a man of a kind and contented disposition. He was always thankful to the Great Spirit for everything he received.

The same disposition was inherited by his eldest son, who had now arrived at the proper age to undertake the cere-mony of the *Ke-ig-wish-im-o-win*, or fast, to see what kind of a spirit would be his guide and guardian through life.

Wunzh, for this was his name, had been an obedient boy from his infancy, and was of a pensive, thoughtful, and mild disposition, so that he was beloved by the whole family. As soon as the first indications of spring ap-peared, they built him the customary little lodge at a retired spot, some distance from their own, where he would not be disturbed during this solemn rite.

In the meantime he prepared himself, and immediately went into it, and commenced his fast. The first few days he amused himself in the mornings by walking in the woods and over the mountains.

While he walked through the woods, he felt a strong desire to know how the plants, herbs, and berries grew,

[1] Canto V.

without any aid from man, and why it was that some
species were good to eat, and others possessed medicinal
or poisonous juices.

On the third day he became weak and faint,[1] and kept
his bed.  He fancied, while thus lying, that he saw a
handsome young man coming down from the sky, and
advancing towards him.  He was richly and gayly dressed,
having on a great many garments of green and yellow
colors, but differing in their deeper or lighter shades.  He
had a plume of waving feathers on his head, and all his
motions were graceful.

"I am sent to you, my friend," said the celestial visitor,[2] "by that Great Spirit who made all things in the sky
and on the earth.  He has seen and knows your motives
in fasting.  He sees that it is from a kind and benevolent
wish to do good to your people, and to procure a benefit
for them, and that you do not seek for strength in war or
the praise of warriors.  I am sent to instruct you, and
show you how you can do your kindred good."

He then told the young man to arise and to prepare to
wrestle with him, as it was only by this means that he
could hope to succeed in his wishes.  Wunzh knew he was
weak from fasting; but he felt his courage rising in his
heart, and immediately got up, determined to die rather
than fail.  He commenced the trial, and after a protracted
effort, was almost exhausted, when the beautiful stranger
said, "My friend, it is enough for once ; I will come again
to try you;" and smiling on him, he ascended in the air in
the same direction from which he came.[3]

The next day the celestial visitor reappeared at the same
hour, and renewed the trial.  Wunzh felt that his strength

[1] Page 54.    [2] Page 55.    [3] Page 56.

was even less than the day before, but the courage of his mind seemed to increase in proportion as his body became weaker. Seeing this, the stranger again spoke to him in the same words he used before, adding, "To-morrow will be your last trial. Be strong, my friend; for this is the only way you can overcome me, and obtain the boon you seek."

On the third day he again appeared at the same time, and renewed the struggle. The poor youth was very faint in body, but grew stronger in mind at every contest, and was determined to prevail, or perish in the attempt. He exerted his utmost powers; and after the contest had been continued the usual time, the stranger ceased his efforts, and declared himself conquered. For the first time he entered the lodge; and sitting down beside the youth, he began to deliver his instructions to him, telling him in what manner he should proceed to take advantage of his victory.

"You have won your desires of the Great Spirit," said the stranger.[1] "You have wrestled manfully. To-morrow will be the seventh day of your fasting. Your father will give you food to strengthen you; and as it is the last day of your trial, you will prevail. I know this, and now tell you what you must do to benefit your family and your tribe. To-morrow," he repeated, "I shall meet you and wrestle with you for the last time; and as soon as you have prevailed against me, you will strip off my garments and throw me down, clean the earth of roots and weeds, make it soft, and bury me in the spot. When you have done this, leave my body in the earth, and do not disturb it, but come occasionally to visit the place, to see whether

---

[1] Page 58.

I have come to life, and be careful never to let the grass or weeds grow on my grave. Once a month cover me with fresh earth. If you follow my instructions, you will accomplish your object of doing good to your fellow-creatures by teaching them the knowledge I now teach you."

He then shook him by the hand and disappeared.

In the morning the youth's father[1] came with some slight refreshments, saying, "My son, you have fasted long enough. If the Great Spirit will favor you, he will do it now. It is seven days since you have tasted food, and you must not sacrifice your life. The Master of Life does not require that."

"My father," replied the youth, "wait till the sun goes down. I have a particular reason for extending my fast to that hour."

"Very well," said the old man; "I shall wait till the hour arrives, and you feel inclined to eat."

At the usual hour of the day the sky-visitor returned, and the trial of strength was renewed. Although the youth had not availed himself of his father's offer of food, he felt that new strength had been given to him, and that exertion had renewed his strength and fortified his courage. He grasped his angelic antagonist with supernatural strength, threw him down, took from him his beautiful garments and plume, and finding him dead, immediately buried him on the spot, taking all the precautions he had been told of, and being very confident, at the same time, that his friend would come to life.[2] He then returned to his father's lodge, and partook sparingly of the meal that had been prepared for him. But he never for a moment

[1] Page 59.    [2] Page 62.

forgot the grave of his friend. He carefully visited it throughout the spring, and weeded out the grass, and kept the ground in a soft and pliant state. Very soon he saw the tops of the green plumes coming through the ground; and the more careful he was to obey his instructions in keeping the ground in order, the faster they grew. He was, however, careful to conceal the exploit from his father.

Days and weeks had passed in this way. The summer was now drawing towards a close, when one day, after a long absence in hunting, Wunzh invited his father to follow him to the quiet and lonesome spot of his former fast.[1] The loop had been removed, and the weeds kept from growing on the circle where it stood; but in its place stood a tall and graceful plant with bright-colored silken hair, surmounted with nodding plumes and stably leaves, and golden clusters on each side.

"It is my friend!" shouted the lad. "It is the friend of all mankind! It is Mondawmin! We need no longer rely on hunting alone; for as long as this gift is cherished and taken care of, the ground itself will give us a living."

He then pulled an ear.

"See, my father," said he, "this is what I fasted for. The Great Spirit has listened to my voice, and sent us something new, and henceforth our people will not alone depend on the chase or on the waters."

He then communicated to his father the instructions given him by the stranger. He told him that the broad husks must be torn away, as he had pulled off the garments in his wrestling; and having done this, directed him how the ear must be held before the fire till the outer

[1] Page 63.

skin became brown, while all the milk was retained in the grain. The whole family then united in a feast on the newly grown ears, expressing gratitude to the Merciful Spirit who gave it.[1] Thus corn came into the world, and has ever since been preserved.

## KWASIND, OR THE FEARFULLY STRONG MAN.[2]

PAUWATING was a village where the young men amused themselves very much in ancient times in sports and ball-playing.

One day as they engaged in their sports, one of the strongest and most active, at the moment he was about to succeed in a trial of lifting, slipped and fell upon his back. "Ha! ha! ha!" cried the lookers-on, "you will never rival Kwasind." He was deeply mortified; and when the sport was over, these words came to his mind. He could not recollect any man of this name. He thought he would ask the old man, the story-teller of the village, the next time he came to the lodge. The opportunity soon occurred.

"My grandfather," said he, "who was Kwasind? I am very anxious to know what he could do."

"Kwasind," the old man replied, "was a listless, idle boy. He would not play when the other boys played, and his parents could never get him to do any kind of labor. He was always making excuses. His parents took notice, however, that he fasted for days together; but they could not learn what spirit he supplicated, or had chosen as the guardian spirit to attend him through life. He was so inattentive to his parents' requests, that he at last became a subject of reproach.

[1] Page 64.          [2] Canto VI.

" ' Ah,' said his mother to him one day, ' is there any young man of your age in all the village who does so little for his parents? You neither hunt nor fish.[1] You take no interest in anything, whether labor or amusement, which engages the attention of your equals in years. I have often set my nets in the coldest days of winter without any assistance from you, and I have taken them up again while you remained inactive at the lodge fire. Are you not ashamed of such idleness? Go, I bid you, and wring out that net which I have just taken from the water.'

" Kwasind saw that there was a determination to make him obey. He did not therefore make any excuses, but went out and took up the net. He carefully folded it, doubled and redoubled it, forming it into a roll, and then with an easy twist of his hands wrung it short off, with as much ease as if every twine had been a thin, brittle fibre.[2] Here they at once saw the secret of his reluctance, — he possessed supernatural strength.

" After this the young men were playing one day on the plain, where there was lying one of those large, heavy, black pieces of rock which Manabozho is said to have cast at his father. Kwasind took it up with much ease, and threw it into the river. After this he accompanied his father on a hunting-excursion into a remote forest. They came to a place where the wind had thrown a great many trees into a narrow pass. ' We must go the other way,' said the old man; ' it is impossible to get the burdens through this place.'[3] He sat down to rest himself, took out his smoking apparatus, and gave a short time to reflection. When he had finished, Kwasind had lifted away the largest pine-trees, and pulled them out of the path.

[1] Page 68.    [2] Page 69.    [3] Page 70.

"Sailing one day in his canoe, Kwasind saw a large furred animal which he immediately recognized to be the king of beavers. He plunged into the water in pursuit of it. His companions were in the greatest astonishment and alarm, supposing he would perish.[1] He often dove down and remained a long time under water, pursuing the animal from island to island, and at last returned with the kingly prize. After this his fame spread far and wide, and no hunter would presume to compete with him.

"He performed so many feats of strength and skill that he excited the envy of the Puck-wudj In-in-ee-sug, or fairies, who conspired against his life.[2] 'For,' said they, 'if this man is suffered to go on in his career of strength and exploits, we shall presently have no work to perform. Our agency in the affairs of men must cease. He will undermine our power, and drive us at last into the water, where we must all perish, or be devoured by the wicked Neebanawaaig.

"The strength of Kwasind was all concentrated in the crown of his head. This was, at the same time, the only vulnerable part of his body, and there was but one species of weapon which could be successfully employed in making any impression on it. The fairies carefully hunted through the woods to find this weapon. It was the bur or seed-vessel of the white pine. They gathered a quantity of this article, and waylaid Kwasind at a point on the river where the red rocks jut into the water, forming rude castles — a point which he was accustomed to pass in his canoe. They waited a long time, making merry upon these rocks, for it was a highly romantic spot. At last the wished-for object appeared. Kwasind came floating

[1] Page 71.    [2] Page 202.

calmly down the stream, on the afternoon of a summer's day, languid with the heat of the weather, and almost asleep.[1] When his canoe came directly beneath the cliff, the tallest and stoutest fairy began the attack. Others followed his example. It was a long time before they could hit the vulnerable part; but success at length crowned their efforts, and Kwasind sunk, never to rise more.

"Ever since this victory, the Puck-wudj In-in-ee have made that point of rock a favorite resort. The hunters often hear them laugh, and see their little plumes shake as they pass this scene on light summer evenings.

"My son," continued the old man, "take care that you do not imitate the faults of Kwasind. If he had not so often exerted his strength merely for the sake of *boasting*, he would not, perhaps, have made the fairies feel jealous of him. It is better to use the strength you have in a quiet, useful way than to sigh after the possession of a giant's power. For if you run, or wrestle, or jump, or fire at a mark only as well as your equals in years, nobody will envy you; but if you would needs be a Kwasind, you must expect a Kwasind's fate."

### MANABOZHO'S FISHING.[2]

His grandmother told him that his grandfather, who had come to the earth in search of her, had been killed by Megissogwon (the wampum or pearl-feather), who lived on the opposite side of the great lake.

"When he was alive," she continued, "I was never without oil to put on my head, but now my hair is fast falling off for the want of it."

[1] Page 204.    [2] Canto VIII.

" Well ! " said he, " Noko, get cedar bark, and make me a line whilst I make a canoe."

When all was ready, he went out to the middle of the lake to fish. He put his line down, saying, —

" Me-she-nah-ma-gwai, — Kingfish,[1] — take hold of my bait."

He kept repeating this for some time.

At last the King of the fishes said, —

" Manabozho troubles me. Here, Trout, take hold of his line."

The trout did so. He then commenced drawing up his line which was very heavy, so that his canoe stood nearly perpendicular ; but he kept crying out, " Wha-ee-he ! wha-ee-he ! " till he could see the trout. As soon as he saw him, he spoke to him, —

" Why did you take hold of my hook? *Esa ! Esa !* — shame ! shame ! — you ugly fish ! "

The trout, being thus rebuked, let go.

Manabozho put his line again into the water, saying, —

" King of fishes, take hold of my line ! "

But the King of the fishes told a monstrous sunfish to take hold of it ;[2] for Manabozho was tiring him with his incessant calls. He again drew up his line with difficulty, saying as before, " *Wha-ee-he ! wha-ee-he !* " while his canoe was turning in swift circles. When he saw the sun-fish he cried, —

" *Esa ! Esa !* you odious fish,[3] why did you dirty my hook by taking it in your mouth? Let go, I say, let go."

The sunfish did so, and told the King of fishes what Manabozho said.

Just at that moment the bait came near the King ; and

[1] Page 82.          [2] Page 83.          [3] Page 84.

hearing Manabozho continually crying out, "Me-she-nah-ma-gwai, take hold of my hook," at last he did so, and allowed himself to be drawn up to the surface, which he had no sooner reached than at one mouthful he took Manabozho and his canoe down.[1]

When he came to himself, he found that he was in the fish's belly, and also his canoe. He now turned his thoughts to the way of making his escape. Looking in his canoe, he saw his war-club, with which he immediately struck the heart of the fish. He then felt a sudden motion, as if he were moving with great velocity. The fish observed to the others, —

"I am sick at my stomach for having swallowed this dirty fellow, Manabozho."

Just at this moment he received another more severe blow on the heart. Manabozho thought, —

"If I am thrown up in the middle of the lake, I shall be drowned ; so I must prevent it."

He drew his canoe, and placed it across the fish's throat;[2] and just as he had finished, the fish commenced vomiting, but to no effect. In this he was aided by a squirrel, who had accompanied him unperceived until that moment. This animal had taken an active part in helping him to place his canoe across the fish's throat. For this act he named him, saying, —

"For the future, boys shall always call you Adjidaumo — animal tail upward."

He then renewed his attack on the fish's heart, and succeeded, by repeated blows, in killing him. This he first knew by the loss of motion, and by the sound of the beating of the body against the shore. He waited a

[1] Page 85.      [2] Page 86.

day longer to see what would happen. He heard birds scratching on the body, and all at once the rays of light broke in. He could see the heads of gulls, who were looking in by the opening they had made.

"Oh," cried Manabozho, "my younger brothers, make the opening larger, so that I can get out."

They told one another that their brother Manabozho was inside of the fish.[1] They immediately set about enlarging the orifice, and in a short time liberated him. After he got out he said to the gulls, —

"For the future you shall be called Kayoshk — noble scratchers or grabbers — for your kindness to me."

The spot where the fish happened to be driven ashore was near his lodge. He went up and told his grandmother to go and prepare as much oil as she wanted. All besides, he informed her, he should keep for himself.

## MANABOZHO AND PEARL-FEATHER.[2]

THE abode of Megissogwon was defended first by fiery serpents, who hissed fire so that no one could pass them; and in the second place, by a large mass of gummy matter lying on the water, so soft and adhesive that whoever attempted to pass, or whatever came in contact with it, was sure to stick there.[3]

Manabozho continued making bows and arrows without number, but he had no heads for his arrows. At last Noko told him that an old man who lived at some distance could make them. He sent her to get some. She soon returned with her *conaus*, or wrapper, full. Still he told her he had not enough, and sent her again. She returned with as many more. He thought to himself, —

1 Page 87.    2 Canto IX.    3 Page 92.

"I must find out the way of making these heads."

Cunning and curiosity prompted him to make the discovery. But he deemed it necessary to deceive his grandmother in so doing.

"Noko," said he, "while I take my drum and rattle, and sing my war-songs, go and try to get me some larger heads for my arrows; for those you brought me are all of the same size. Go and see whether the old man cannot make some a little larger."

He followed her as she went, keeping at a distance, and saw the old artificer at work, and so discovered his process. He also beheld the old man's daughter, and perceived that she was very beautiful.[1] He felt his breast beat with a new emotion, but said nothing. He took care to get home before his grandmother, and commenced singing as if he had never left his lodge. When the old woman came near, she heard his drum and rattle without any suspicion that he had followed her.

After having finished his term of fasting and sung his war-song, — from which the Indians of the present day derive the custom, — he embarked in his canoe, fully prepared for war. In addition to the usual implements he had a plentiful supply of oil. He travelled rapidly day and night; for he had only to will or speak, and the canoe went.[2] At length he arrived in sight of the fiery serpents. He stopped to view them. He saw they were some distance apart, and that the flame only which issued from them reached across the pass. He commenced talking as a friend to them; but they answered, —

"We know you, Manabozho; you cannot pass."

He then thought of some expedient to deceive them,

[1] Pages 50, 51.     [2] Page 93.

and hit on this. He pushed his canoe as near as possible.
All at once he cried out, with a loud and terrified voice, —

"What is that behind you?"

The serpents instantly turned their heads, when, at a
single word, he passed them.

"Well," said he placidly, after he had got by, "how
do you like my exploit?"

He then took up his bow and arrows, and with deliberate aim shot them.[1] This was easily done; for the serpents
were stationary, and could not move beyond a certain spot.
They were of enormous length, and of a bright color.

Having overcome the sentinel serpents, he went on in
his canoe till he came to a soft, gummy portion of the
lake, called Pigiu-wagumee, or Pitch water. He took the
oil, and rubbed it on his canoe, and then pushed into it.
The oil softened the surface, and enabled him to slip through
it with ease, although it required frequent rubbing,[2] and a
constant reapplication of the oil. Just as his oil failed, he
extricated himself from this impediment, and was the first
person who ever succeeded in overcoming it.

He now came in view of land,[3] on which he debarked
in safety, and could see the lodge of the Shining Manito,
situated on a hill. He commenced preparing for the fight,
putting his arrows and clubs in order; and just at the dawn
of day began his attack, yelling and shouting and crying,
with triple voices: "Surround him! surround him! run
up! run up!" making it appear that he had many follow-
ers. He advanced, crying out: "It was you that killed
my grandfather;" and with this shot his arrows.

The combat continued all day. Manabozho's arrows
had no effect, for his antagonist was clothed with pure

---

: Page 94.        [2] Page 95.        [3] Page 96.

wampum.[1] He was now reduced to three arrows, and it was only by extraordinary agility that he could escape the blows which the Manito kept making at him.

At that moment a large woodpecker, the Ma-ma, flew past, and lit on a tree.

"Manabozho," he cried, "your adversary has a vulnerable point. Shoot at the lock of hair on the crown of his head!"

He shot his first arrow so as only to draw blood from that part. The Manito made one or two unsteady steps, but recovered himself.[2] He began to parley, but in the act received a second arrow, which brought him to his knees. But he again recovered. In so doing, however, he exposed his head, and gave his adversary a chance to fire his third arrow, which penetrated deep, and brought him a lifeless corpse to the ground.

Manabozho uttered his *saw-saw-quan;* and taking his scalp as a trophy, he called the woodpecker to come and receive a reward for his information. He took the blood of the Manito, and rubbed it on the woodpecker's head, the feathers of which are red to this day.[3]

After this victory he returned home, singing songs of triumph, and beating his drum. When his grandmother heard him she came to the shore, and welcomed him with songs and dancing. Glory filled his mind. He displayed the trophies he had brought in the most conspicuous manner, and felt an unconquerable desire for other adventures. He had destroyed the Manito of Wealth, and killed his guardian serpents.[4]

But his feats and adventures do not terminate here. There is scarcely a prominent lake, mountain, precipice,

[1] Page 99.    [2] Page 100.    [3] Page 101.    [4] Page 103.

or stream in the northern part of America which is not hallowed in Indian story by his fabled deeds.

To collect all these and arrange them in order would be an arduous labor; and, after all, such an arrangement would lack consistency and keeping, unless much of the thread necessary to present them in an English dress were supplied by invention, alteration, and transposition.

How long Manabozho lived on earth is not related. The period of his labors and adventures having expired, he withdrew to dwell with his brother in the North,[1] where he is understood to direct those storms which proceed from points west of the pole. He is regarded as the spirit of the northwest tempests, but receives no worship from the present race of Indians. It is believed by them that he is again to appear, and to exercise an important power in the final disposition of the human race.


## IAGOO, THE GREAT BOASTER.[2]

IAGOO is the name of a personage noted in Indian lore for having given extravagant narrations of whatever he had seen, heard, or accomplished.[3] He always saw extraordinary things, made extraordinary journeys, and performed extraordinary feats. He could not look out of his lodge and see things as other men did. If he described a bird, it had a most singular variety of brilliant plumage. The animals he met with were all of the monstrous kind; they had eyes like orbs of fire, and claws like hooks of steel, and could step over the top of an Indian lodge. He told of a serpent he had seen which had hair on its neck like a mane, and feet resembling a quadruped.

[1] Page 242.    [2] Canto XI.    [3] Page 117.

Iagoo did not appear to have been endowed with the ordinary faculties of other men. His eyes appeared to be magnifiers, and the tympanum of his ears so constructed that what appeared to common observers to be but the sound of a zephyr, to him had a far closer resemblance to the noise of thunder. His imagination appeared to be of so exuberant a character that he scarcely required more than a drop of water to construct an ocean, or a grain of sand to form an earth.

Notwithstanding all this, there are but a few scraps of his actual stories to be found. He first attracted notice by giving an account of a water lilly [*sic*], a single leaf of which, he averred, was sufficient to make a petticoat and upper garments for his wife and daughter. One evening he was sitting in his lodge, on the banks of a river; and hearing the quacking of ducks on the stream, he fired through the lodge door at a venture. He killed a swan that happened to be flying by, and twenty brace of ducks in the stream. But this did not check the force of his shot; they passed on, and struck the heads of two loons, at the moment they were coming up from beneath the water, and even went beyond and killed a most extraordinary large fish called Moshkeenozha.

On another occasion he had killed a deer, and after skinning it, was carrying the carcass on his shoulders, when he spied some stately elks on the plain before him. He immediately gave them chase, and had run, over hill and dale, a distance of half a day's travel, before he recollected that he had the deer's carcass on his shoulders.

One day, as he was passing over a tract of mushkeeg, or bog land, he saw mosquitoes of such enormous size that he staked his reputation on the fact that a single wing of one of the insects was sufficient for a sail to his canoe, and the proboscis as big as his wife's shovel. But he was favored with a still more extraordinary sight in a gigantic ant which passed him, as he was watching a beaver's lodge, dragging the entire carcass of a hare.

### OSSEO, OR THE SON OF THE EVENING STAR.[1]

THERE once lived an Indian in the North who had ten daughters, all of whom grew up to womanhood.[2] They were noted for their beauty, but especially Oweenee, the youngest, who was very independent in her way of thinking. She was a great admirer of romantic places, and paid very little attention to the numerous young men who came to her father's lodge for the purpose of seeing her.

Her elder sisters were all solicited in marriage from their parents, and one after another went off to dwell in the lodges of their husbands or mothers-in-law; but she would listen to no proposals of the kind. At last she married an old man named Osseo, who was scarcely able to walk, and was too poor to have things like others. They jeered and laughed at her on all sides; but she seemed to be quite happy, and said to them, —

"It is my choice, and you will see in the end who has acted the wisest."

Soon after the sisters and their husbands and their parents were all invited to a feast; and as they walked along the path they could not help pitying their young and handsome sister, who had such an unsuitable mate. Osseo often stopped and gazed upward; but they could perceive nothing in the direction he looked, unless it was the faint

[1] Canto XII.      [2] Page 129.

glimmering of the evening star. They heard him muttering to himself as they went along; and one of the elder sisters caught the words, —

"*Sho-wain-ne-me-shin nosa* — pity me, my father."[1]

"Poor old man," said she, "he is talking to his father; what a pity it is that he would not fall and break his neck, that our sister might have a handsome young husband."

Presently they passed a large hollow log lying with one end toward the path. The moment Osseo, who was of the turtle totem, came to it, he stopped short, uttered a loud and peculiar yell, and then dashing into one end of the log, he came out at the other a most beautiful young man; and springing back to the road, he led off the party with steps as light as the reindeer. But on turning round to look for his wife, behold! she had been changed into an old, decrepit woman, who was bent almost double, and walked with a cane. The husband, however, treated her very kindly, as she had done him during the time of his enchantment, and constantly addressed her by the term of *ne-ne-moosh-a*, or my sweetheart.

When they came to the hunter's lodge with whom they were to feast, they found the feast ready prepared; and as soon as their entertainer had finished his harangue (in which he told them his feasting was in honor of the Evening or Woman's Star), they began to partake of the portion dealt out. The food was very delicious; and they were all happy but Osseo, who looked at his wife and then gazed upward, as if he was gazing into the substance of the sky.[2] Sounds were soon heard, as if from far-off voices in the air; and they became plainer and plainer, till he could clearly distinguish some of the words: —

<hr/>

[1] Page 131.     [2] Page 133.

" My son — my son," said the voice, " I have seen
your afflictions, and pity your wants. I come to call you
away from a scene that is stained with blood and tears.
The spell you were under is broken. Ascend, my son —
ascend into the skies, and partake of the feast I have prepared for you in the stars, and bring with you those you
love.

" Your bowls and kettles shall be no longer wood and
earth. The one shall become silver, and the other wampum. They shall shine like fire, and glisten like the most
beautiful scarlet. Every female shall also change her state
and looks, and no longer be doomed to laborious tasks.
She shall put on the beauty of the starlight, and become
a shining bird of the air, clothed with shining feathers.
She shall dance, and not work — she shall sing, and not
cry."

The words were intelligible to Osseo; but his companions thought them some far-off sounds of music, or birds
singing in the woods. Very soon the lodge began to shake
and tremble, and they felt it rising into the air. It was
too late to run out, for they were already as high as the
tops of the trees. Osseo looked around him as the lodge
passed through the topmost boughs, and behold ! their
wooden dishes were changed into shells of a scarlet color,[1]
the poles of the lodge to glittering wires of silver, and the
bark that covered them into the gorgeous wings of insects.
A moment more and his brothers and sisters and their
parents and friends were transformed into birds of various
plumage. Some were jays, some partridges and pigeons,
and others gay singing-birds, who hopped about display-
ing their glittering feathers. But Oweenee still kept her

[1] Page 135.

earthly garb, and exhibited all the indications of extreme age.

He again cast his eyes in the direction of the clouds, and uttered that peculiar yell which had given him the victory at the hollow log. In a moment the youth and beauty of his wife returned; her dingy garments assumed the shining appearance of green silk, and her cane was changed into a silver feather. The lodge again shook and trembled; and they immediately after found themselves in the Evening Star, the residence of Osseo's father. . . .

Osseo lived happy and contented in the parental lodge; and in due time his wife presented him with a son, who grew up rapidly, and was the image of his father. He was very quick and ready in learning everything that was done in his grandfather's dominions; but he wished also to learn the art of hunting, for he had heard that this was a favorite pursuit below.[1]

To gratify him, his father made him a bow and arrows; and he then let the birds out of the cage, that he might practise in shooting. He soon became expert, and the very first day brought down a bird; but when he went to pick it up, to his amazement it was a beautiful young woman, with the arrow sticking in her breast. It was one of his younger aunts. The moment her blood fell on the surface of that pure and spotless planet, the spell was dissolved. The boy immediately found himself sinking, but was partly upheld by something like wings, till he passed through the lower clouds, and he then suddenly dropped on a high, romantic island in a large lake. He was pleased, on looking up, to see all his aunts and uncles following him in the form of birds; and he soon discovered the

[1] Page 139.

silver lodge, with his father and mother, descending, with its waving barks looking like so many insects' gilded wings. It rested on the highest cliffs of the island, and here they fixed their residence.[1] They all resumed their natural shapes, but were diminished to the size of fairies; and as a mark of homage to the King of the Evening Star, they never failed, on every pleasant evening during the summer season, to join hands and dance on the top of the rocks. These rocks were quickly observed by the Indians to be covered, on moonlight evenings, with a larger sort of Puk-wudj In-in-ees or little men, and were called Mish-in-e-mok-in-ok-ong, or turtle spirits; and the island is named from them Michilimackinac to this day. Their shining lodge can be seen in the summer evenings when the moon shines strongly on the pinnacles of the rocks, and the fishermen who go near those high cliffs at night have even heard the voices of the happy little dancers.

## PAUGUK.[2]

PAUGUK is the personification of death. He is represented as existing without flesh or blood. He is a hunter, and besides his bow and arrows is armed with a pugga-magon, or war-club. But he hunts only men, women, and children. He is an object of dread and horror. To see him is a sure indication of death. Some accounts represent his bones as covered by a thin, transparent skin, and his eye-sockets as filled with balls of fire.

Pauguk never speaks. Unlike the Jeebi, or ghost, his limbs never assume the rotundity of life, neither is he to be confounded in form with the numerous class of minor

[1] Page 140.     [2] Page 220.

Manitoes, or spirits. He does not possess the power of metamorphosis. Unvaried in repulsiveness, he is ever an object of fear; and often, according to Indian story, has the warrior, flushed with the ardor of battle, rushing forward to seize the prize of victory, clasped the cold and bony hand of Pauguk.

## CANTO XI.

### *HIAWATHA'S WEDDING FEAST.*

#### THE SONG OF CHIBIABOS.

##### *Page 125.*

A CORRESPONDENT of *Littell's Living Age* (vol. xxv., 1850, p. 45) gives the Indian serenade and a literal transcription which Longfellow put into the mouth of Chibiabos: —

Onaiweh! Paikesai! meteequen, quonadhj cuskanosd musco-
    taiwenin.
Onaiweh! Onaiweh! kepahshoshe mocaiseheeon.
Taupai kaisainopemayan, mannenatuk azhenah pahkesaikew
    taupai containen ai won.
Nodin keokeneta waikon azhenah menoqut paike saiwen oske-
    nega kez heeudwaikon azhenah menoquten pawwepemuk-
    kazho, nahgoosing.
Nekaugewahnahtahsee neshainonen ahehewaukie, azhenah mok-
    keet chewun kerhiz alchew au washeekoseekazho?
Nemeetah nug gamha taupai keeshiah payshoo azhenah aske-
    noga meteequen weneemenin nodin oteihaiminkazho.
Taupai nescaudizhe saugittewun, nemeetah muccuddahwah az-
    henah wabbiskah se bewun waupai nahcut endosh wainje
    ishpenning.
Ketiyahnin geozhetone menoaedum nemeetah sunnag gezenin

azhenah kezhis geoshetone azhenah azauwoshsheneah
tegowugninse kissenah nodin wainjenetahhahwajink.
Neahwena wahhundummo keshainon nemeetah pokkaumenin.
Ah ke tahyahnin nepeesh tahyahnin ishpenning tahyahnina,
    kooshah nanah — yehah kaykekendun mekunnuh tahyah-
    nah mokeshee taupai kaukesshiah — Onaiweh ! Onaiweh !
    nenah saugittewun.

### LITERAL TRANSLATION OF THE ABOVE.

Awake ! flower of the forest — beautiful bird of the prairie.
Awake, awake ! thou with the eyes of the fawn.
When you look at me I am happy ; like the flowers when they
    feel the dew.
The breath of thy mouth is sweet as the fragrance of the flow-
    ers in the morning ; — sweet as their fragrance at even-
    ing in the moon of the fading leaf.
Does not the blood of my veins spring towards thee, like the
    bubbling springs to the sun — in the moon of the bright-
    est nights ?
My heart sings to thee when thou art near ; like the dancing
    branches to the wind, in the moon of strawberries.
When thou art not pleased, my beloved, my heart is darkened
    like the shining river when shadows fall from the clouds
    above.
Thy smiles cause my troubled heart to be brightened, as the
    sun makes to look like gold the ripple which the cold
    wind has created.
Myself ! behold me ! — blood of my beating heart.
The earth smiles — the waters smile — the heavens smile, but I
    — I lose the way of smiling when thou are not near —
    Awake, awake ! my beloved.

He thus remarks : "I send you an Indian serenade.
The Indian language, however hard to pronounce in English, and however harsh it seems when *we* endeavor to

pronounce it, is very sweet and silvery, or rather *liquid* (to express it more correctly), when spoken by an Indian. It flows softly and melodiously from their lips. One reason is (I think), the superior modulation of voice, so much more extended and graceful. In pronouncing a word the voice passes from one key to another as softly as in singing, and at the same time passes through a greater number of notes. In a word, there is less monotony of tone. The accompanying song seems to be a mixture of the Ottawa and Ojibway (or Chippewa), which are dialects of the same language, and differ but slightly. What is very singular, the Indians find it difficult to pronounce the soft sound of our *l*, and have it not in their language. The *r* they cannot pronounce — their tongues seem formed to prevent it. Their language is capable (*I think*) of being formed into a grammar, though it has never been done. So far as I have examined it, it accords with certain fixed principles. There are certain words and expressions, used by one or the other sex, not used in common. For instance, their expression of surprise or astonishment is the same in Indian that it sometimes is in English ; viz., ' O my ! ' used by both man and woman ; but the man says, ' T'ya,' while the woman says, ' N'ya,' — one signifying the male, the other the female. For a man to use the ' N'ya ' is considered extremely effeminate, while it is the height of presumption in the woman to say ' T'ya.' ''

## ODJIBWA SONG.[1]

IN 1759 a Chippewa girl, named Paig-wain-e-oshe-e, or White Eagle, met at the Lake of Two Mountains a young

[1] Page 142.

Algonquin belonging to the French mission. They fell in love; and she is said to have composed the following song, the first stanza of which in the original runs thus: —

> Ia indenaindum,
> Ia indenaindum,
> Ma Kow we yah,
> Nin denaindum we,
>   O dishquadumee.

### I.

Ah me! When I think of him, — when I
think of him — my sweetheart, my Algonquin.

### II.

As I embarked to return,
he put the white wampum round my neck —
a pledge of truth, my sweetheart,
my Algonquin.

### III.

I shall go with you, he said —
to your native country —
I shall go with you, my sweetheart,
my Algonquin.

### IV.

Alas! I replied —
my native country is far, far away,
my sweetheart, my Algonquin.

### V.

When I looked back — where we parted,
he was still looking after me,
my sweetheart, my Algonquin.

### VI.

He was still standing
on a fallen tree — that had fallen
into the water, my sweetheart,
my Algonquin.

### VII.

Alas! when I think of him —
When I think of him —
It is when I think of him,
my Algonquin!

This song, evidently inaccurately translated, is found in Schoolcraft's *Onéota* almost immediately following the tale of Shingebis the Diver (page 23). Longfellow puts it most gracefully and almost unchanged into the mouth of Chibiabos in Canto XII.

VI.

He was still standing
on a fallen tree — that had fallen
into the water, my sweetheart,
my Algonquin.

VII.

Alas! when I think of him —
When I think of him —
It is when I think of him,
my Algonquin!

This song, evidently inaccurately translated, is found in
Schoolcraft's Oneóta almost immediately following the
tale of Shingebis the Diver (page 221). Longfellow puts
it most gracefully and almost unchanged into the mouth
of Chibiabos in Canto XII.